Applause For
SHEDDING THE CORPORATE BITCH

Funny, gut wrenching, and inspiring... a great read.
> — **Greg Reid**, speaker, filmmaker and author of
> *Think and Grow Rich, Three Feet from Gold*

Bernadette Boas really puts herself out there to help other women succeed where she didn't. Her openness and vulnerability in Shedding the Corporate Bitch *was moving.*
> — **Gail Evans**, author of *Play Like a Man, Win Like a Woman*

I love Bernadette's message that to be successful you don't need to be anything more than who you are right now. Authenticity matters.
> — **Dr. Paula Fellingham**, CEO, The Women's Information Network (The WIN)

Bernadette Boas takes a hard look in the mirror and discovers insights that she now shares with us in black and white for others to learn from. Most important, because Bernadette has been there, done that, you will have first-hand, "up close and personal" real world experience that can only be had by the trial and error method of the school of hard knocks. I highly recommend her new book for the successful businesswoman inside all of us!
> — **Linda Wind**, CEO, Wind Enterprises and Founder, Wind Foundation for Women and Emerge! Scholarships, formerly The Possible Woman Foundation Intl.

Thank you, Bernadette, for your vulnerable authenticity, that reveals the healing necessary in any leader—male or female, who wants to lead with integrity. After decades of helping businesses transform to get results they did not even think possible, it is clear it is this deep inner work that is at the core of powerful results.
> — **Roxanne Emmerich**, author of *Thank God Its Monday!: How To Create a Workplace You and Your Customers Love*, and CEO of The Emmerich Group, Inc.

Shedding the Corporate Bitch deals with the very real issues that women have faced to achieve success in business. Ms Boas's revealing insights will prove invaluable for anyone who has struggled with compromising their own identities in order to gain acceptance and beat the odds to achieve success.

— **Patrick Smyth**, CEO, business navigator and author of
Elephant Walk: Business and Brand Strategy for the Long Haul, and
Powering the Wave: A Simplified System to Build and Manage a Business

Shedding the Corporate Bitch *and Bernadette proves that women should not 'Man-up' to succeed in business. Bernadette's insights are moving and yet very logical. This is a must read for all women in business.*

— **Joyce Bone**, author of
Millionaire Moms-The Art of Raising a Business and a Family at the Same Time

Shedding the Corporate Bitch *is touching and funny yet hits you in the gut with Bernadette's revealing hurts and pains she both created and experienced. This book is both a great business book and a great insightful workbook that provides helpful tips toward empowerment and personal growth. I would highly recommend this book to any professional businesswoman whose ambition is to climb the corporate ladder or is in business for themselves.*

— **Rico Pena**, author of *The Client Nation: Their Perception, Your Profits*

Bernadette Boas not only has the courage to change, but she also has the courage to share her journey, her mistakes, and her regrets. We can all learn from her in this insightful, sometimes humorous, and well-written book. I highly recommended this for all women considering a business career or in a business career.

— **Mary A. Madden**, Chair and Executive Director Atlanta Chapter of the
National Association of Corporate Directors and Cofounder,
CEO, and President, Information America, Inc, listed on the Inc. 500.

In a world where many have to reinvent themselves, Bernadette's book shines with the light of hope. It tells us we can be a better person and be happier than we were in the past. It offers words of support for all who are in transition, and encouragement for those who want to move toward their potential.

— **Linda Bishop**, CEO of Thought Transformation,
author of *Selling in Tough Times*

I know that it takes three things for any person to change their mind-set and behavior—Becoming Self-Aware, Being Willing to Make a Change and then Taking Action. Bernadette Boas shows in Shedding the Corporate Bitch *that she did all three magnificently, fearlessly and with great humor and insight. This is a powerful book for all women - especially for those in the business world.*

— **Barbara Taylor**, partner, JanBara & Associates and co-author of
Critical Success Factors for Leaders in Tough Economic Times

Shedding the Corporate Bitch *will help both women and men to orchestrate the ingredients of success in Corporate America and in life.*

— **Hugh Ballou**, The Transformational Leadership Strategist

Bernadette Boas offers a brave account of an identity that many women have embraced and the breaking down of that untruth to reveal the real woman of power deep within. Being a bully, a bitch or heartless is no longer necessary. In fact, it is merely another mask often worn to disguise deeper pain. Bravo for revealing the bitch persona and the road to reclaiming oneself!

— **Maria Gamb**, author of *Healing The Corporate World*

Bernadette has the energy, humor, and clarity of thought to share life lessons from which we can all benefit. Her dedication to helping other women by sharing her story is evident throughout the book.

Women must often walk a fine line between showing their decisive, commanding leadership presence and being called a bitch. Dancing on this razor's edge has consequences, and each woman must make a choice for herself as to what types of behavior work for her. Her version of success is a decision each individual woman must make. Bernadette shows us her journey and the lessons she has learned can guide others.

— **Jane Lowenstein**, co-author of
Critical Success Factors for Leaders in Tough Economic Times

For all of us corporate "bitches" out there, this is a great book that you can really sink your teeth into. Too often women let their job consume their lives and define themselves. Bernadette Boas' Shedding the Corporate Bitch *teaches us how to take care of ourselves and to focus on what really matters in life—not our work or obligations or to-do lists, but our dreams and passions. With her insights and strategies, we can quickly shed our negative attitudes and triumph in life with happiness, pure joy, inner peace, and self-love.*

— **Becky Boyd**, MediaFirst PR

Bernadette Boas discovers insights that she now shares in concrete and practical terms for others to learn from. Shedding the Corporate Bitch *is a must-read business book for women who feel pressured to adopt competitive and unauthentic management styles in order to climb the career ladder of success. Providing helpful tips, Bernadette's book will remind businesswomen everywhere that we can be ourselves and still succeed!*

— **Barbara Giamanco**, co-author of
The New Handshake: Sales Meets Social Media and CEO of Talent Builders, Inc.

SHEDDING THE CORPORATE BITCH

Shifting Your BITCHES to RICHES in Life and Business

BERNADETTE BOAS

NEW YORK

SHEDDING THE CORPORATE BITCH
Shifting Your BITCHES to RICHES in Life and Business

Bernadette Boas

ISBN 978-1-60037-940-6 Paperback
ISBN 978-1-60037-941-3 E-Pub Version
Library of Congress Control Number: 2011922093

Published by:

Morgan James Publishing
The Entrepreneurial Publisher
5 Penn Plaza, 23rd Floor
New York City, New York 10001
(212) 655-5470 Office
(516) 908-4496 Fax
www.MorganJamesPublishing.com

Foreword by
Dawn Walls Bain PHD

**Illustrations for interior
& front cover by**
Havana Nguyen of
Havana Graphics

Cover Design by:
Rachel Lopez
rachel@r2cdesign.com

Interior Design by:
Bonnie Bushman
bbushman@bresnan.net

In an effort to support local communities, raise awareness and funds, Morgan James Publishing donates one percent of all book sales for the life of each book to Habitat for Humanity.

Get involved today, visit
www.HelpHabitatForHumanity.org.

To my Mother and my rock, Mary A. Boas

And in loving memory of my Father and my hero, George L. Boas

NOTE FROM AUTHOR

Welcome to the inner sanctums of shedding the bitch—whatever that angst, attitude or negative mindset may be.

I hope you enjoy reading Shedding the Corporate Bitch and learning from my own successes and pains. If you are able to take away any tips, lessons, or impacts to your own life, I would love to hear from you via feedback, comments, blog postings and your own stories. You may find for yourself that you can impact one other person as well.

Here's to your discovery, shedding and the creation of a wonderful life for yourself!

Enjoy,
Bernadette Boas

CONTENTS

FOREWORD

By Dawn Walls Bain PHD

We peel onions. We shuck corn. Snakes shed their skin. So, how do you shed a Corporate Bitch? We can shed our coats, our socks, our shoes, and at times, even shed a few pounds! So again, how does one shed a Corporate Bitch?

We are not born a "bitch", unless of course you are a female puppy. Webster defines bitch as a female dog. Hmmm. Since we humans are not dogs, why do we find "bitch" so easily attributed to powerful women?

Bernadette Boas spent her career perfecting the ultimate bitch image... and to you that is Ms. Corporate Bitch. Just as a doctor is proud to see the MD, so was she proud of her accomplishments in climbing the corporate ladder. While working at one of her first jobs in Boca Raton, Florida, she was shown this bitch persona by a wealthy woman she was serving. She observed that through having a nasty, demanding and degrading attitude, this rich woman could get anything she wanted! By being nasty! The richer—the more "bitch-i-er" was what she was being shown. It was then that Bernadette decided she wanted a life of power and riches. Her compelling story of personal hardship and growth will have you laughing and crying.

Bernadette was raised in a loving and supportive family. Being nasty was just not part of her formative years. Therefore, throughout her corporate years of accumulating wealth and status, her family was supportive of her career dreams but also concerned about her lifestyle. Something had to change. Something dramatic was going to happen. It did. You are not going to believe what happened on the day she heard, "You're fired."

Through her experiences of "Corporate Bitchdom" and nastiness, to eventually coming out on the other side of hateful, Bernadette shares with you how she learned forgiveness, compassion, truth, and the ability to let go of what was not serving her in her life.

What is it that drives this insatiable desire to become "someone" in this world of ours? In a word, it is the wish for *POWER*. With it, we believe we are elevated above a crushing world of others who want at all costs what we want—to end their struggle with fear. Without it, we feel not only unprotected, but unremarkable. Our daily affairs seem to have little to no meaning, because we're sure no one recognizes our *WORTH*. It is this unconscious and unchallenged conclusion that drives men and women to the point of collapse. Let's put it this way: We have not been running *to* something—that goal or that dream—as much as we have been running *from* the fear of being NO ONE. This is a race we can never hope to win, because we are tied to whatever we avoid. What we resist—persists. This also explains why, so far, our fear has determined our race through life. The good news is that even though this search for POWER over our fear is as old as humanity itself… so is the real solution. Ours is the task of discovering that our TRUE nature has nothing to do with fear. Start by challenging the false notion that "negatives" or "nastiness" or "bitch-i-ness" are true powers. Deliberately walk past any circumstance where painful presence—left uncontested—makes you a prisoner of its domain.

As Bernadette states: it's ALL about me—the Real "ME" of course. Shed the Bitch and see.

Rev. Dr. Dawn Walls-Bain, Metatuitive
CEO of Blue Dawn Marketing, Enchanted Forest Press, and Metatuitive Moguls
Published Author of: *Ageless Wisdom for Modern Business*

INTRODUCTION

As I lay on the ground of Memorial Park, a wave of humiliation and disgust washed over me. I couldn't move. Charlie stood over me, trying to catch his breath.

Park-goers strolled by, afraid to stop, but called out as they walked past, "Are you okay?" I tried to grasp the magnitude of the truth that had smacked me in the face as I quietly jogged around the two-mile park. All of the events which had occurred since my self-proclaimed day of independence—losing my job, walking away from a six-figure salary, giving up my big title—swirled in my head.

All my life, my family, friends, and colleagues had seen me as a strong, confident, successful, and adventurous woman. I saw myself as all of these things, too. Yet, there I was, lying on the ground of a public park, realizing that I was none of them, at least not in the way all those people saw it. Simply put, I had lived every day of my adult life as a bitch. I had caused so much pain and heartbreak to my family, friends, and colleagues.

Realizing these things about myself was painful. It is also what made me want to write this book. I wanted to apologize to all the people throughout my life who I may have hurt in any way. I wanted to account for my bitchiness and take responsibility for any of the outcomes which had come about as a result. And I wanted to help others live the life they were born to live. I was convinced that if I could use my story to help other people, I would have achieved that goal.

I was determined to take accountability and responsibility for all of the pain I had caused in my life.

I stood up and brushed the dirt from my backside.

I picked up Charlie's leash to finish my run. Over the next several weeks and months, I found myself digging deep into my soul and my past; reliving episodes, encounters, and interactions, personal and professional. I relived all of the hurts and pains, all of the insecurities and intimidations, and all of my successes and failures in hopes of forgiving myself and helping others. Eventually, I faced the bitch in the mirror and finally made the shift to who I am today.

Through all of this discovery and recovery, I have learned that I am the most successful and happy being I was born to be. I have shed the corporate bitch persona and uncovered the real me—a beautiful, bold, audacious, and successful woman. I want the same for you.

Your "bitch" is any virus of the spirit or soul which suffocates and wants to kill off the real you. It could be as challenging as dealing with cancer, divorce, menopause, or raising kids, or as tragic as a death. A "bitch" can be born when dealing with bad habits like smoking or dieting, and as scary as tackling a new sport, new job, or even a new relationship. Unfortunately, the smallest of negative mindsets and the biggest 'I can't do it' belief system will create the 'bitch' that prevents you from pursuing your goals and dreams and achieving the riches of life.

My goal in sharing my story, while protecting the real names of those involved, is to show you that living a life that is true to you, that puts YOU first, and that allows you to be the best YOU that you can be, is the most powerful, healthy, and wealthy way to live. ***I want to help you shift from bitch to rich!***

"Once upon a time there were two bitches, one called L. and one Bernadette B. They both worked for a very big name in the U.S. Both had nothing better to do but micro-manage, play games, be "loud" and fire people....fortunately and finally the company realized that both bitches were just a "waste of time" and the bitches finally had to bite the dust. One bitch though now claims to have all the answers...perhaps she should reflect on herself and be totally honest, she may as well realize that she is the biggest bitch?!"

— Actual email from a disgruntled, former employee of Bernadette Boas, which was submitted in response to an anonymous request for stories about nightmare bosses.

"Do you have any idea how hurtful you are to people?" Linda asked. She shook her head and did everything she could to avoid eye contact with me.

I looked across the room at Sheila, searching for some validation of what Linda had said. All I could see was her slumped in her chair, sitting silently as Brian talked in her ear.

Over the years, I rarely thought about how my bitch affected the people around me. I didn't think about it because I didn't care. I really believed that the way I went about my life was the right way, the most effective way, to get what I wanted. No one was telling me otherwise, so I continued lashing out, venting, condescending people, disrespecting them, and being a bitch to anyone who crossed my path.

If anyone had told me I was being a bitch, I wouldn't have believed it. In fact, most times, people who inflict pain have no idea they are doing it. Or they do not care enough to think about it. I admit I was both of these; I didn't know and I didn't care, until the walls came crashing down around me.

As I stood in the parking lot following the latest blow-out with my former boss about a major account, sweat ran down my face, the hairs on my arms stood on end, and my heart raced like a train. I feared I was having a heart attack. If ever there was a moment God had spoken to me, this was it. Right then and there, I decided that no amount of money or power was worth losing my life. I would put my ambitions into other passions that would not inflict pain on the world.

And if I could apologize to all of the women and men on whom I afflicted pain, embarrassment, or disappointment, I would. In fact, I will apologize, now:

Forgive me for the bitch I was.
Forgive me for not knowing that I was.
Forgive me for not caring that I was.
I am truly sorry.
— **Bernadette Boas**

Chapter 1

INDEPENDENCE DAY

I woke up, looked in the mirror, and wondered, *who is this person staring back at me?* I shivered and turned away.

I certainly never dreamt that one day, the person staring back at me in the mirror would be one whom I neither understood nor liked. *What happened to the young, precocious, and sassy girl I was once?* I am not sure how I became that person, but I do know exactly when and where I was when I decided I wanted no more of her. It was a mind-blowing, life-altering moment for me.

We all have those moments in life which we can recall with exact precision of time and place. Moments where in one split second, everything changed forever. In my own life, I've had three of those. The first was August 16, 1977, the day Elvis died. I had just finished a swim at the local pool and country club when I heard the news. I stood, frozen, as the announcement blared from the radio at the registration desk. I waited for someone to admit it was just a big joke.

It happened again on July 16, 1999, when I walked into my neighborhood nail salon looking forward to a relaxing foot massage and pedicure. When I walked in, the TVs around the room delivered the news that JFK Jr. and his wife, Carolyn, had crashed their plane into the Atlantic and were presumed dead. "Are you kidding me?" I wondered aloud. "This can't be true." What American woman didn't love, or at least lust for, John Jr.? Just like his father and uncle before him, he was gone too soon.

I also recall July 29, 1981. On that beautiful, summer day, I sat with hundreds of other college kids on the floor of the dorm lobby, riveted to the TV, as Princess Diana prepared to say her vows to Prince Charles. I remember every detail of that glorious, jeweled gown with a train that seemed to go on for miles. What young girl doesn't dream of being swept off her feet by Prince Charming? And I vividly remember the day, sixteen years later, on August 31, 1997, when I returned to my apartment after a night on the town with friends and switched on the TV to hear the unthinkable: Princess Diana had died in a horrific car crash in the tunnels of Paris. Lady Di, the stunningly shy "People's Princess," was dead. *This can't be happening*, I thought. Shocked, I crumbled to the floor and sobbed.

Those events played a significant role in my life because they involved people whom I admired, and the events themselves shook me to the core. November 26, 2007, was no different. That was the day my circumstances—and my life—completely changed, forever. It was my personal Independence Day.

It was the Monday after a fun-filled Thanksgiving holiday weekend which I'd spent hanging out with friends and overindulging in everything from food and drink to football. That day began like any other. The alarm buzzed at 5:30 a.m. I awoke to a slightly chilly fall day which was heavy with the smell of damp leaves in the air. Weary and in a fog, I leapt out of bed and into the shower. I blew out my mop of curly red hair, downed a fast oatmeal, and sprinted out the door to kick-start the week. My mind raced faster than a jet engine. I had a standard weekly status meeting with my boss, Doug. But these days, Monday morning meetings approached like unwelcome houseguests.

I was one of several global vice presidents within the technology company where I worked, and for the last few months we had all led extremely hectic lives. My team was about to deploy a couple of major worldwide initiatives, which several division heads of the company had fought against from day one. I had two candidates scheduled to interview for a director's opening whose budget had not yet been confirmed. On top of that, the company had just spun apart from its parent organization, creating a whole new paradigm of leadership. The entire leadership team was feeling the pressure of proving to Wall Street that we could stand on our own as a profitable powerhouse in the technology industry. That pressure had begun to trickle down to all of management and their teams, including mine.

I got into my car and drove northbound on I-85, reinvigorated from the long weekend. My mind wandered as I drove along the mostly empty interstate, a rarity in Atlanta, where traffic is notoriously deadlocked, especially on Monday mornings. That's why I always left my house no later than 6:30 a.m. At that time of morning, the highways were nearly always empty and I could complete the eighteen mile drive to work in about fifteen minutes.

As I drove north toward the office, I wondered if the gang would show up at their normal, late, post-holiday hour or if, like me, they would rush into the office to get a jump on the piles of work that sat on their desks. I pulled into the parking lot to find only a couple of cars already there. I greeted the guards at their post and headed to my office to prepare for my meeting. I loved getting to work early, before the halls filled with people racing from office to office. I savored the quiet—no people chatting, no copiers running, no phones ringing.

When I reached my office, I picked up my papers and notepad and walked down the long hallway to the corner conference room at the front of the building. I took a deep breath and looked out at the main parking lot and the entrance to the building. I watched the mad rush of employees coming to work, the double-parked UPS truck dropping off shipments, and food distributors delivering goods to the cafeteria.

I sat quietly, imagining scenarios about the other employees who now passed through the building's entry doors. I pictured them leaving their homes each morning, kissing their spouses and children goodbye, yelling at other Atlanta drivers on the highway, and racing into the parking lot to get a prime spot near the front door.

My thoughts wandered to the single man and woman whom I'd seen leaving from the same office during lunch or at the end of the day. Were they going right home or looking for a private place between here and there to rendezvous?

These days, a great number of the people who left our 5,000-plus-employee technology company throughout the day would never return. Jobs, even teams, vanished as a result of corporate restructuring. Sitting in this very seat, I watched folks exit those front doors for the last time. They looked shocked and angry, even fearful. Where would they go once they drove out of the parking lot? Where would they end up? When would they find another job?

As a manager, I'd had to let a number of people go over the years. I hated it, but it was business. Still, I caught myself wondering where I would go and what I would do if I were fired from a company where I had worked for the last eleven years of my life. I shuffled and re-organized the papers in front of me.

By 8:00 am, Doug had still not shown up. This was unusual for him, but I wasn't concerned, given the previous holiday weekend. He finally waltzed in at 8:15. I was enjoying the view outside and the fantasies that were dancing around in my head. When he sat down, I jumped right into multiple project updates—those that were on time, delayed, or had serious deployment issues.

Doug abruptly cut me off and without hesitating, repeated the words I'd said many times through the years: "We have to talk." If you have ever heard or delivered those words to anyone, you know that nothing good follows. My heart sank. I stared directly at him.

"Your position is being eliminated." he continued. "You would have an opportunity, of course, to……blah, blah, blah, blah, blah." I didn't hear another word. Everything went quiet, except for that deep, muffled sound you hear when you plunge underwater. I could hear Miss Othmar, Linus' teacher from the Peanuts; say, "Woh, woh, woh, woh, woh". I licked my dry lips and attempted to smile.

My heart raced like a railroad train, and yet, I felt strangely calm and peaceful.

Doug paused. He studied me, never once blinking. I could tell from his eyes that he did not know what was going on. I'm sure he wondered why I was being so quiet. His face turned red and his eyes darted back and forth. He looked nervous and confused, as though waiting for me to explode.

Where was the fighter, the bitch, that I was known to be? The one who would raise royal hell and fight hard for what she believed? The one who would argue with someone just for the sake of it? He moved his chair an inch away from the table. Did he fear that I'd reach across the table and smack him? Doug knew me to never back down from a fight and yet at this very critical, life-altering moment, I was motionless, not responding at all in the way he'd come to expect.

The silence lingered. Someone down the hall was brewing a pot of coffee and the smell wafted through the air. Doug began to sway back and forth in his chair and started to talk again. I cut him off. "Doug, you don't need to continue. I get it," I said. He stopped, stunned. I was stunned myself. *Why wasn't I fighting?* I continued to talk, with a hint of giddiness in my voice. "I know a lot of changes are going on, and I am not surprised that this is happening to me," I continued. "I just need you to take care of the two director candidates waiting in the front lobby for their interviews with me." While I spoke, I gathered my note pads and papers and left the conference room.

As I raced through the now-busy, noisy halls, I wished I had eyes behind my head. I imagined Doug in his seat, mouth gaped, grateful to have escaped a typical "Bernadette bitch-out".

I rushed toward my office and felt a laugh rise inside my throat. I thought, *Oh my God! On the very morning I was pumped up and ready to hit the ground running, thinking about all the other employees coming and going from this building, I have been let go.* I was the one with no job. It sounded so bizarre, all I could do was giggle.

Even more bizarre, my job was eliminated on the very morning I was scheduled to interview candidates for the director's position I had created. *Did Doug not know this was going to happen today? Why would he have me fly folks in from around the country, have them show up on the Monday morning after a holiday weekend, and then before 9:00 a.m., eliminate the hiring manager and all of her direct report positions? What were they thinking?* It was actually funny, I thought, giggling again.

After 25 years witnessing the inner-workings of corporate restructurings, it didn't surprise me, and more importantly, it was no longer my worry. I took a deep breath and quickened my pace down the hall. My mind spun in all different directions. I felt some excitement, some anxiety, and some disbelief. But strange as it sounds, I felt great!

I tossed my collection of personal items, pictures of my family and Charlie, a coffee mug, and sales and leadership awards I'd earned over the years into a large satchel. Without a word, I headed down the main hall of the building and out the same set of doors through which I had watched people come and go only minutes earlier. It was 8:30 a.m. It had taken exactly thirty minutes for me to become one of those people I had fantasized about. I wondered who might be watching me from the big window, imagining where I'd go and what I'd do next. Wow! The impact of what had just happened finally hit me. *I just lost a lucrative, six-figure, executive- level job with a company I had been with for over a decade.* I had given this company loyalty, dedication, hard work, nights and weekends, and even tears. I was their most loyal sergeant, always at attention and ready to answer the call of duty. *How could they? Did they not realize what they were losing? Did they not care?* I felt a twinge of anger well up inside me. But, just as quickly, it disappeared.

I finally reached my car. I turned around, keys in hand, and looked back at the office building that I had come to every day for eleven years, knowing that my team and Doug, who had just fired me, went on with their day. I tried to make sense of the strange feelings that had taken over me. I didn't feel anger, nor was I hurt. Instead, I felt an unbelievable sense of weightlessness. It was like a 500-pound elephant had just fallen off my back. I suddenly felt lighter, freer, and calmer than I could remember. Actually, I *couldn't* remember ever feeling this way.

I got into my car, looked back again at the office building, and drove out of the parking lot for the last time. As I drove back down I-85, I braced myself for the explosion of anger that had become my trademark. But it didn't come. Instead, I focused on the yellow leaves which still clung to the trees lining the interstate. I remembered the weekend laughter. I heard my mother's soothing, reassuring voice whisper, "You will be just fine, honey".

"It is what it is," I sighed.

Thirty minutes later, I found myself in another parking lot, twenty miles from my now former office. This parking lot was full of cars and people going to their morning workouts. I stopped in front of the Cumberland LA Fitness, a local gym where many of my friends worked out the stresses of their day.

Maybe a workout is what I need right now, I thought. Nah! I was feeling giddy and wanted to share that excitement with someone. I knew exactly who that 'someone' was.

My friend, Holly, is the most predictable, compulsive, person I know. I knew that at 9:00 a.m. I would find her at this very gym, sweating up a storm climbing a Stairmaster or riding a bike.

I had met Holly two decades ago at another gym, the Olympiad, in Boca Raton, Florida. At the time, she was a tall, healthy, slim size 8. Her 5' 9" frame was always small and lean, with not even a trace of fat. About twelve years into our friendship, during a day of jean shopping, her body image changed drastically. I'm not sure if she ever realized it, but I certainly did.

I was desperate for a pair of jeans, but because I'd worked in retail for years, absolutely hated clothes shopping. Fortunately, Holly loves to shop; she loves to help me spend my money even more. So one sunny Saturday afternoon, we made our way to Ann Taylor Loft for the tortuous ritual of trying on pair after pair of jeans, trying to find the one that fit just right.

Rummaging through the racks, we pulled out several pairs and sizes to try on. I had been working out hard and looked forward to showing off in my new jeans. Holly worked out regularly herself and her body showed it. But during that shopping trip, we discovered something we had never even considered before: we were now the same size. Although Holly was tall and lean, and I am only 5'5" with more of an athletic frame, we both wore the same size 8.

As I modeled the jeans and asked her opinion on how they looked, she said, "You may need a smaller pair. What size are they?"

"Size 8," I replied. The look on her face caught me completely off guard.

"No way! You can't be," she scowled. How could I, with my thicker, more muscular legs and waist, fit into the same size jeans as her long, thin legs? Sure, the lengths of jeans were always a tricky matter for both of us, but from her response, you would have thought I had called her a fat cow.

I'm not sure if Holly ever consciously realized what happened that day, but almost immediately, she began a compulsion of daily workouts and a diet fit for a bird—only lettuce, cottage cheese, and watered down wine. She went from a healthy size 8 to a frail size 2—and has stayed that way ever since. Holly's physical and emotional reaction to my response was very hurtful to me. It was as though she was calling *me* the fat cow. The hurt dissipated long ago, but what transpired on that day is branded on my memory forever.

As I sat in the gym parking lot, I felt like I had already been up and going for days. But it was only 9:30 a.m. Holly's schedule had not changed for years, and I knew she wouldn't be done with her class or stair climbing until at least 10:00 or 10:15. I sat in my car and let my body sink deep into the driver's seat. After all, I had no place to go, just all the time in the world.

As I sat there, excited and anxious, I began to process everything happening around me. I watched a mom fussing over her baby in a stroller, a young woman adjusting her workout bra as she walked into the gym, and a guy sorting through his trunk full of gym supplies.

Denial, I thought. *Am I in denial?* That's one of the stages of grief, I had learned. Maybe that's why I didn't feel anger. Maybe I was in denial and anger would come later.

But everything in my body and soul screamed "freedom," not denial, nor anger. My mind raced with all kinds of crazy ideas about what my next step would be. I shook my head, as if trying to shake out the mental noise, and turned on the radio to an adult contemporary music station. I closed my eyes, sat still, and waited.

I caught a glimpse of Holly leaving the gym and heading toward her car. She had no clue that I was sitting in my car, parked directly behind hers. She would never expect me to be here on a Monday morning.

She climbed into her large Toyota Sequoia. She sat so high up in her SUV, my Lexus sedan suddenly felt like a two-door Miata. She pulled out of the lot onto Cumberland Parkway. I followed right behind her like a jilted lover stalking his mistress. *Will she notice I'm right behind her?* I wondered. No way. Holly is so predictable; she assumes everyone else is, too. The only place she would ever expect me to be at 10:00 a.m. is at my corporate job—my "big job," as she saw it. I prayed she was going directly home and not on to run errands at Target, TJ Maxx, Marshalls and Publix, as she did nearly every day. I didn't like the idea of pouring my heart out in public.

Her car turned and headed up the parkway toward her townhouse. As I followed close behind, I dialed her number on my cell. After a couple of rings she shrieked, "What's up?" noticing my number on her caller ID.

"I'm following right behind you," I said.

"Get out of here!" she shouted, adjusting her rear view mirror to catch a glimpse of me. I waved at her. "Are you kidding?" she asked. She slammed on her brakes, nearly causing me to rear-end her. Holly never liked surprises. She has a time, plan and routine for every aspect of her life, and any disruptions to that can cause her and those around her, including me, a great deal of stress.

Her voice took on a completely different tone, a concerned one.

"What's wrong? Is your family okay? How's your mother? What's happened?" she rattled off. It could never be just a surprise visit, like, "Hey, I just decided to take the day off." Okay, she knew better. Up until that morning, my career had been everything to me. Goofing off was not an option.

"Yes, everything is fine with my family," I said. "It's nothing bad. I just lost my job," I said, matter-of-factly. She didn't say a word. I imagined her eyes wide, jaw dropped. "Let's talk when we get to your house."

Over the years, two things were constant between Holly and me. One, corporate was my life and therefore, my identity. Two, she would never imagine me walking away from the money, position, and power it provided. Status and material things were very important to her too.

The biggest difference between the two of us is that although we both love having money, nice shiny toys, and beautiful houses, I've always wanted to obtain these things for myself. But Holly has always anticipated a man would provide them for her, even though she has always had a job and works her ass off.

We couldn't get to her house fast enough. I imagined her shock and confusion. She wanted to know the scoop and I wanted to get it off my chest. When we reached her house, she opened the garage door, slammed on her brakes, jumped out of her car and opened the door to her house. We didn't say a word until we got inside, found a comfortable seat in her living room, and were sipping on bottled water.

I sat on her couch, crossed my legs Indian-style, and poured out my heart. I replayed every word, feeling, and reaction from that morning as if it had happened to someone else. She listened, scowling, as usual, and shook her head. Sometimes, I wonder why I even come to her with these types of discussions. I always know how she'll respond.

My words contained no anger, spite, or denial. But I did shed some tears. After all, I had just lost my job, my identity, my *purpose*. It was a big loss, like a death or divorce, and I cried as the reality set in. But it was my laughter that really got to Holly.

Finally, she said, "You are awfully giddy for having just been fired from a job and a company that you have loved for so long. What is that about?" I laughed at the irony of it all and shook my head.

"I know, right?" I replied.

She didn't say another word. She didn't have any. Holly avoided difficult conversations about friends going through hard times like the plague. She never engages in them. It hasn't been any different since the day we met.

When Holly and I met in Boca Raton, we were both in our mid-to-late twenties and in very different social circles. What we had in common was the gym and the people we knew from the gym. It was completely coincidental that we both ended up in Atlanta.

In 1984, Holly wanted a change and figured Atlanta could be that change—and if it had more men than South Florida, even better. I had worked directly with a retail company in Atlanta and was able to hook her up with an interview and eventually a job. One year later, I would be transferred to that same company. The workplace, people and social circles formed the tie that would keep our friendship together. Those ties lasted for years, even though our relationship lacked the transparency, intimacy, and vulnerability upon which most friendships are based.

After more than twenty years, I can count the number of deep, involved discussions Holly and I have ever had. No matter how serious the issue— whether it was about men, my near-rape by a cop, the death of my father, or the number of times life caused us to butt heads with one another— there was never a discussion about it. When there was, it amounted to, "Are you okay?" "Yes, I am." "Good." That was it. Arguments? No such thing. Breakdowns? Tears? No way. We had what I would call a surface friendship, never an emotional connection. It was like many family relationships, where you love your relatives, no matter what.

I explained to Holly how I sat in the conference room, imagining other folks being laid off and leaving those halls for the last time. *Happy* for them, *scared* for them, *praying* for them. And just minutes later, it was happening to me. "Why do I keep laughing?" And then it hit me. I realized that I could finally leave behind a part of me that I had been dying to let go of for so long, probably for years.

From the look on Holly's face, I wasn't sure if she got it or if she thought I was totally crazy. I knew she would never understand, or even agree with, my decision to walk away from it all. And that was okay. I didn't expect her to.

After 25 years working for and reporting to someone else, working on the projects and with the customers they dictated, and on a schedule they gave me, I finally had the chance to call the shots. I could decide who I wanted to work with, what I wanted to do, and where I would do it. I would finally be able to do something for myself, on my terms; without the politics, boardroom games, boys' club, or other people's agendas.

For the first time, I would have a chance to be me, the *real* me, the *authentic* me. I could shed the persona I had taken on and allowed to live inside me for reasons I was unable to articulate at that moment. I realized that the sudden weightlessness, the feeling of calm and peace running through my bones, signaled the death of the person I'd learned to become on my way up the corporate ladder.

I had to deal with how I had gotten to this point. How and why I had allowed myself to journey so far away from my true self, to take on a persona of a *bitch*, and what influences had brought me to this point? I would have to dig deep and take responsibility for my decisions and behavior. I knew it wouldn't be easy and certainly not fun to work through, but I said to myself, "Bring it on, all of it, I dare ya!" Now is *my* time! This is *my* Independence Day!"

Neither Holly nor I said much more. I relished my newfound freedom, and I left her with her opinions.

Chapter 2

THE CALM BEFORE THE STORM

I'm not sure what I did or where I went after I left Holly's at noon on that eventful day.

When I finally pulled up to my house, my dog, Charlie, was sitting at the back door, anxiously awaiting my return. The antique clock on the kitchen wall read 4:00 p.m. After such an emotional day, it was just great to be home. Charlie greeting me with a big wet lick across my face made it that much better.

Charlie played a prominent role in my decompression. I needed to work through my emotions and what better way to do that than a game of fetch? My poor dog nearly wore himself out chasing tennis balls, racing up and down the slate steps, and bouncing off the brick walls that frame our multi-level, fenced-in back yard. I fell to my knees, laughing hysterically as I watched him slide across the slippery, moss-covered ground, leap high in the air to snatch the flying ball, and try to chase a squirrel up a tree. His goofy grin did more for me than a whole bottle of Prozac ever could—not that I'd ever attempt to find that out!

When we finally went inside, Charlie headed straight for his water bowl, slurping some but leaving most of the water on the floor. Afterward, he headed to the living room and leapt onto couch. Like a kid who calls, "Shotgun!" before a car ride, Charlie immediately laid claim to his side of the couch. He has done that since the day I brought him home.

You could say he dominated the couch. No one dared sit in, stand over, or even think about taking his precious spot. If they did, my 80-pound Labradoodle baby would jump into their lap and wiggle back and forth until they took the hint and moved to the left side of the couch. Stretching out proudly, Charlie would look at me with a big, wide grin and raised eyebrows as if to say, "Told you so. This is *my* house and *my* spot. Nah, nah, nah, nah, nah, nah."

I returned to the yard to clean up the squeaky tennis balls, tug toys, and rope ties he'd strewn everywhere. When I went back inside, I went right to the wine cooler, picked out a pinot noir, poured myself a glass, and made my way to the couch. Charlie was still in his spot, pretending to be asleep. I took my side of the couch and laughed out loud as I pulled the large, beige, chenille blanket over us. I switched on the TV and stared at the images on the screen.

There wasn't a single show that could keep me awake. I leaned on the glass top of the wood frame cocktail table and pushed myself slowly up from the couch. Charlie awoke immediately when I said, "Nightie-night". Moments later, he was out again, this time snoring at the foot of the bed, his head resting on my feet.

On any other night, I found comfort in Charlie using my legs, stomach, or feet as a pillow. But tonight, his weight felt like a ton of bricks. Five, ten, thirty minutes had passed, and I was still awake. I pulled the covers up to my chin and burrowed closer to Charlie.

At 11:14, I was still staring at the ceiling. At 12:20, I nearly fell out of bed, scared to death, when my neighbor's Labradors started barking. The noise echoed inside my head. I reached over to the night stand and pulled out my ear plugs and eye mask.

These sleep aids were tokens of my now-defunct corporate life. In more than twenty years traveling overseas and around the country, I'd collected quite a few of these goodies, as well as fluffy socks, headphones, and facial wipes. These little trinkets had helped to make many a long, boring flight more comfortable. Tonight, I prayed they would help silence the noise inside my head and send me off to dreamland.

The ear plugs created a tunnel-like vibration in my head, like crashing ocean waves. My breathing and heart rate slowed. My eyelids began to feel heavy and my body went limp under Charlie's weight. Still conscious of my breathing, I watched several flashes of light streak across the black canvas of my closed eyelids. The streaks lit up like fireworks in a Fourth of July sky.

Before long, the streaks of lightning became an onslaught of surreal images and ideas. In one image, I saw myself standing on top of a mountain, dressed in all white, arms outstretched, hair blowing in the wind. I felt so free, it was like an out-of-body experience. A few minutes later, I was at the bow of a ship, with waves crashing down over me and I was laughing.

These images gave glimpses into the possibilities that lay ahead. *What would my future be? Where would I go?* I wondered. *Would I leave Atlanta?* "No way!" I said out loud, remembering how I'd come to Atlanta in the first place.

I spent my childhood and teenage years in Philadelphia. After high school, I moved to Boca Raton, Florida, where I attended Florida Atlanta University. Corporate life came calling and I remained there for another ten years. Despite my mother's endless promptings, I had made up my mind that I was never moving back to Philadelphia. Only when I obtained my residency and sent her my paperwork did she accept that her precious little girl was never coming home.

Later, when I made the decision to leave Boca, my friends thought I was crazy. "It's so beautiful here," they said.

"Yes, Boca Raton is a beautiful city, indeed," I'd agree. "But trust me, a beautiful city does not guarantee happiness - not at all."

I found my next home, my last home, my *real* home—Atlanta, Georgia—in July 1994. It was Charlie's home now, too. Moving was definitely not an option. As ideas and possibilities continued to light up my mind, I realized I was open to anything but a move from my beloved city.

Sleep continued to elude me. *I could be a standup comedian*, I thought. I replayed the first and only stand-up gig I had ever done. I actually got up in front of a crowd of 200 at Atlanta's Punchline Comedy Club and absolutely loved it! Don't get me wrong, it was scarier than hell. I compare it to the way people must feel on their first bungee jump. You stand there on the edge, ready to jump, praying that you don't hit the ground.

Maybe I'll be a singer, I thought. *No way!*

People have said my deep, raspy voice would be great for the radio, but I'm more of a screamer than a singer. I'll leave singing to my sister, Peggy. Though we have very similar speaking voices, she is the one who sounds like Barbra Streisand, not I.

As a teenager, I wanted to run off to Paris and be an artist. I was quite good. As a young girl, I was rarely seen without my sketch pad and pencils. Once, at Disney World for our family vacation, I squatted on the curb of Main Street in the Magic Kingdom, ready to sketch anyone who would let me. I watched in awe as the official Disney World caricaturists and portrait artists sketched the faces of the guests who paid to sit for them.

For me, Main Street was my Paris. It was lined with cafés and gift shops, filled with tourists with cameras hanging around their necks, and cluttered with children screaming with delight as they rode the many rides. My dreams of being a Disney artist faded when Main Street employees sidelined my efforts to convince guests to pay me a quarter to sketch them. Years later, I travelled to Paris. By then, I was posing for my own caricature, the one I had become.

Maybe I would stick to what was safe and easy for me and take another corporate executive or management type of job. The projects, people, and companies provided me everything I was looking for—title, position and money. Plus, I was really good at what I did. But the mere thought turned the butterflies in my belly into bees, causing me to feel physically ill.

The ideas continued to run in front of me like an endless river. I yanked off the ear plugs and eye mask. It was clear that I was not going to drown out the fury raging inside my head. I nestled up against Charlie in hopes that maybe feeling and listening to his slow, deep breathing would put me into a meditative trance. It didn't. The night dragged on.

I have never been the type to get out of bed and read a book or watch television when I can't sleep. Although there are books on each of the three tables in my room, there is no television. Usually, when I'm lying awake in bed unable to sleep, I plan for the next day. There's a tape recorder and journal on my nightstand in case a great idea wakes me up in the middle of the night. By the time the morning alarm buzzes and I fly out of bed, I have a game plan in hand, ready to tackle the day. Lying alone in bed in the middle of the night, I have little else to do besides talk into a recorder or scribble in a journal.

Tonight was different in so many ways. Sitting up quietly in bed, propped up by pillows, I envisioned what tomorrow would bring. I grabbed the recorder and began to recite all the things I needed to accomplish the next day. *I need to call Doug*, I thought, *and discuss what next steps I need to take.* Then, reality hit me: *hell, I don't need to call Doug. I don't ever need to call him again.*

"Tomorrow I don't have anywhere to go," I shrieked, waking Charlie. "It's okay Boo, go back to sleep," I whispered, as I pulled the blanket over his head.

What a strange and exhilarating feeling! For the first time in more than 25 years, I had absolutely nowhere to go in the morning. No business suit to put on, no presentation to prepare, no meeting plan for. I had no heavy lifting or work to do. Not for anyone or anything. Not for tomorrow, next week, or next month. I was, for the first time in my entire life, completely free of any responsibilities. I tossed the recorder back onto the nightstand and crawled back under the covers.

I felt as if an alien had taken over my body. I felt so at peace. The burdens of deadlines, employees, vendors, bosses, and customers vanished. The wielding of authority, power, demands, and direction melted away. Just days ago, I had been attacking every project or activity with perfectionism, urgency, and Type A obnoxiousness. I couldn't remember a time when I had nothing to do or nowhere to go.

Before today, I had thrived on being busy and stressed out. The bigger the risk, the bigger the pressure, the more I liked it. The more critical the project, the better I performed. Tell me I could lose my job if something didn't happen like it should, and it would fuel my determination and success. Yet, here I was in the middle of a cold, fall night filling my sleepless hours with my new to-do list; when to walk the dog, what to make for lunch, and when I'd schedule my two-mile run.

No wonder I couldn't sleep. My entire life had changed today. Drastically.

I felt that 'punch drunk' exhaustion where your energy is depleted, your mind screams for quiet and you feel as if you could cry at the drop of a pin. I pleaded with God for sleep. As the clock ticked away—midnight, one, two— my pleas became more desperate. "Please, I need to sleep!" I whimpered. "I know you're listening," I pleaded, as tears trickled down my cheeks.

It was not a matter of *if* it would happen, but *when*. When I would find myself in an all-out panic attack. When the reality hit that my long-standing career and financial security were gone, just like that. When it would hit me that a business family I had known and cared about for over a decade was suddenly no longer there. When I would miss the access to authority and power I'd had over projects, people, and resources. How can you be a bossy bitch with no one to boss around?

For years, I had thrived and depended on all of those things. They gave me purpose and in many ways defined me. Okay, I'll admit the six-figure salary wasn't bad, either. It afforded me a couple of different houses, a nice car, a great wardrobe, quarterly visits to see my family in Philadelphia, and vacations around the world, without ever looking at a price tag. Because I was single and childless, my salary gave me many freedoms and lots of ego.

Anyone who had known me since my early twenties knew how important title, power, and position were to me. It was written all over my face and reflected in my attitude.

On this first night of freedom, I had trouble imagining what it would be like not directing large groups of people, not heading up important strategic projects, not taking responsibility for critical decisions and risks. I loved the exhilaration of sitting in a boardroom with a group of smart, ambitious people hashing out business issues. We weren't eradicating world hunger, but it sure felt like we were. Everyone seated at that table fought for their solution, their perfect idea, their position. We'd play power games like people played Monopoly—strategic and ruthless. I never cared if things got heated or nasty. I thrived on the tension; the more confrontational, the better. Life wasn't fun without drama, and for many years it wasn't fun unless I'd made someone feel less smart or worthy than me. I shuddered as that thought raced through my mind.

Would anyone miss me? I laid back and wondered. I imagined my team members crying over my departure and my mentors and bosses storming into the CEO's office demanding my return. I smiled at the images of my many corporate customers tearing up all future contracts with the company if I was not reinstated.

But deep down, I wondered if anyone would really care. What about Bob, my closest colleague, or my team member, Linda? How about Donald? Is this something he really supported? Surely they'd miss me. My head began to spin again. As much as I cared about the answers to these questions, I was too tired to worry about them now.

I glanced over at Charlie, whose body twitched and eyes flitted back and forth as he slept. I felt a strong sense of connection to him. I had never appreciated his warmth as much as I did in that very moment.

My eyes grew heavy. Finally, blackness filled the room.

At 5:30 a.m., the alarm buzzed and I sat straight up in bed. Grasping for comprehension and clarity, I wondered what day it was. I quickly grabbed the cell phone from the end table to silence the alarm. Squinting, I saw that the alarm had not been set. I climbed over Charlie to the other end table to hit the button on the clock radio, but that alarm had not been set, either.

The alarm, that was ringing, was in my head. It had awakened me this morning, as it had every morning for the last 25 years. I felt like Bill Murray in the movie, *Groundhog Day*. In the film, Murray's character wakes up every morning, day in and day out, at the same time, triggered by the same sounds. It took just seconds for me to decide to lay back down and go back to sleep. I felt as if I had been hit by a Mac truck.

Charlie was still buried under the covers and didn't move an inch as I squirmed back under the covers. I wrestled to get my legs from under his, wanting to stretch out straight on my side of the bed. Charlie always found a way to claim the entire width of the queen size bed. This morning, I was clinging for dear life to the edge of the mattress, praying I wouldn't fall to the floor. With one big push, Charlie was on his side of the bed.

Minutes later, Charlie and I were snoozing and dreaming once again. My dreams took me back to yesterday morning, when Doug said the words, "We want you to find another job elsewhere in the company."

What? How dare they? My blood had started boiling the minute Doug uttered those words. *Really? He wanted me to go out into the company and search for another job—and do it myself. Are you f*** kidding me?* I thought. *Does he really think that after all these years working my ass off, I was going to look for a job with less title, position, and money? Is he crazy?*

I had never searched for a job. All three major companies, I had worked for since college, had recruited me. Even promotions and raises came with few interviews. I worked hard at every job I ever had and was damn good at what I did. That is not attitude, it's a fact. Now, more than twenty years later, I was being told that not only was I losing the job that I loved and worked my ass off for, but I had to search for another job within a company where I had already proven myself.

Everyone who knew me knew I would never take a step backward in any part of my life. Sure, I may give up money or even title and position, but only if there was a bigger payoff. It certainly wasn't going to be for lesser pay, title, or responsibility. And yet, that's what staying with the company would have meant. I wouldn't understand the real reason behind it for some time.

Chapter 3
THE BITCH REVEALED

Wednesday came and went without any new mental light shows. So did Thursday and Friday. My days were free of the worry, anxiety and pressures of my former corporate life. By the time Saturday morning came, my body and mind had adjusted to a new wake up time—8:00 a.m. When the buzzer rang, I leapt from bed, free and weightless, ready for a long run around Memorial Park. Charlie sprang to his feet, expecting a road trip or playtime with his friends. He was right.

The morning temperature was in the low 40's, unusually cold for that time of year. As much as I enjoyed running, it didn't always like me, evident from the strain on my knees and throbbing muscles in my legs. The cold temperatures aggravated both of these conditions. Although I believe in working out, I don't believe in torturing myself, especially in the cold, rain, or unbearable Atlanta heat. Still, I was anxious to get out on the road and shake the noise from my head.

I bundled myself up in mis-matched running and cycling gear scraped together from my closet: long Under Armour running pants, a Nike turtle neck thermal top and running jersey, and a Gore windbreaker. I piled on the layers, knowing I could always shed clothing if I got too hot.

When we reached the park, it was packed. There was a steady stream of children, strollers, runners, and cyclists all trying to get their workout in on that chilly morning. With so many people in the park, Charlie would have to run on his leash, making my run more challenging than usual.

Charlie and I had a routine when we arrived: he would jump out of the car, run for the nearest bush, relieve himself, and proceed to sniff "hello" to anyone who walked past him. I'd then click his leash hook and he would sit down, allowing me to leash him. Finally, we'd set off on a two-mile run around the park.

The blast of cold air whipped against my face and hands and I realized I had forgotten my gloves. I could handle my face getting cold, but I was a big baby when it came to my hands. This morning, they froze as soon as I started running, so I had to run with them, and Charlie's leash, in my pocket. It would not be easy to control Charlie on his leash in this manner, so I prayed my hands would warm up before he saw a squirrel or another dog and tear off in pursuit of the poor, furry creature. Around mile two, I settled into the cold, relaxed my mind and body, and actually forgot about my hands, still tucked inside my windbreaker pockets.

The cold air puffed from my nose in frosty, white billows. The brisk weather was helping to clear my mind of all distractions, including the people running and walking past me, the screaming kids on the swings, and the cars speeding by. I decided to use this time to work through some of the ideas and thoughts that had lit up my sleepless nights over the past week.

I imagined sitting with my sister, Patricia, and filling her in on everything going on. She would ask, "Why are you so calm, content and confident about losing your career? It's been your life!" She'd be right. It had been.

Then I began to think about those once-in-a-lifetime encounters we all experience at some point; the events that rock your core and cause you to come face to face with a "God's speaking" moment. The moment when you just "know" things are about to change, and that change will be the best thing for you, if you listen closely enough to hear it.

It could be the instant you fall in love. Or the moment you know that you want to marry the man standing in front of you. It might be when you say, "Yes," to that big promotion that will take you and your family across the Atlantic. Maybe it's the moment you learn you're pregnant and decide to have the baby, even though you're unmarried.

Throughout my life, I have had many 'God's speaking' moments. I always knew, deep in my soul, when change was coming, and I knew the change was going to be good for me, even when it was painful. Because I knew it was the right change at the right time, I accepted it without fear, doubt, or resistance, like the time I received a call about my father.

It was 2005 and I was living in Atlanta. I was meeting a group of friends for dinner, after a nasty falling out had caused us to go our separate ways a year earlier. I was surprised and happy when my friend, Patty, called and asked if I wanted to join the gang for dinner. I told her I'd be happy to, even though, secretly, I dreaded the drama that often accompanied this group's gatherings.

I often felt like I was back in high school with all the petty teenage games: girl likes boy, boy likes girl, friends are jealous, boy finds someone new, friends butt in, fighting breaks out, feelings are hurt, backs are turned, and everyone refuses to discuss it. The inevitable outcome: the girl, in this case, me, gets left behind, becomes bitter toward the world and them, and lashes out by drinking too much and crying too much.

That night, as we sat around the table, I began to feel lightheaded. Shivers shot up and down my spine. The hairs on my arm stood straight up. Without even thinking, I blurted, "A change is coming!" I looked up to see all five of my friends staring at me.

"What change?" Matt asked.

"I don't know, but it's coming," was all I could say.

At that moment, I was convinced that God was speaking to me. A change *was* coming and I was going to need to listen. Less than a week later, on a business trip to North Carolina, God sent His message. I received a call from my sister, who told me my father was being sent home from the nursing facility into hospice care. He was expected to die within two days. Change had definitely come and there would be great pain before there was happiness, but I was prepared for it.

God had warned me of impending change many times throughout my life. I consider them my "God's speaking" moments. Each time, the change felt right. Like now, when everything should have felt uncertain, I felt only calm, content, and confident.

I continued to run, Charlie panting beside me. I envisioned a giant, blank whiteboard, and scribbled what I would eventually call my "3 C's of change": calm, contentment, and confidence. These words would become my mantra. I would start each day chanting and affirming that mantra, in hopes that it would stay with me. I would affirm that this new-found freedom and my 3 C's would lead me to where I was meant to be and who I was to become, making me happier than I have ever been.

The butterflies that continued to flutter in my stomach took flight with the possibility of change. My breathlessness was a sign of anticipation, and my 3 C's were the manifestation of God's blessings and my faith in Him.

My family and friends were caught off guard by my 3 C's. Concerned about my financial security, my future, and my opportunities, they called non-stop the first week. Most, like my sister, Patricia, would ask the logical questions: "What are you going to do next? Are you okay to take care of yourself until you find something else? "What are you most concerned about?"

My so-called friends would make the asinine comments like, "The job market is tough, especially for someone your age," or, "What were you thinking, leaving your job before you had another one?" I was learning who my real friends were by their reaction to the calm, contentment, and confidence I was feeling about my loss. I wasn't upset about it; why were they?

What they never considered was that my 3 C's were catching me off guard too. There wasn't a minute that I didn't question my reaction to this life-altering event. I just decided that rather than fighting and questioning it, I would leverage it to the fullest. It was clear to me that there was something to the way I was feeling and the manner in which I was walking and running through the days following my firing. I believe there is a reason for everything, and my ever-growing belief in fate, destiny, and purpose all stemmed from my faith in God, so there was little questioning on my part.

I was not so naïve as to think I'd never again be overcome by fear, especially since I no longer had an income. My bank account had already begun to dwindle. Surely, there would be days when the thought of losing my home would creep into my mind. After all, I'm only human, and no amount of faith would free me from all concern and doubt.

The temperature was warming up, and I removed my windbreaker and wrapped it around my waist. Mile three came quickly and surprisingly easy. I didn't feel the throbbing in my legs or the pounding in my chest. During most of my runs on very cold days, my one-hundred forty pound frame felt like a thousand pounds. With every breath of cold air, my heart and lungs felt like they were freezing over. I felt the stinging and burning throughout my body. It was a sensation similar to the one you get after pulling your hand quickly from a freezing lamp post. If you're a runner, you know the feeling.

Today's run was definitely one of my best. It was like many drives I had taken up and down I-85, where I would reach my destination and try to remember how I got there. Today, I was logging miles, but neither my body nor my mind was feeling it. I turned my attention from running back to my 3 C's. I feared if I didn't, my feet and legs would surely quit on me.

Charlie began to nip at my arm sleeve as we continued our run, pleading, *"Please mom, can we stop now?"* Although he's part Lab, he does not like to run or chase balls unless I coerce him. And although he's part Poodle, he doesn't like to swim. But he sure is one heck of an actor! After he nips at my sleeve, he'll drag his tongue on the ground, making it difficult for me to run. He knows that by panting like he's having a heart attack and about to keel over dead, I'll stop running—even if it's only been five minutes. It took me a few months to figure out his tactics and they don't work anymore.

So we continued running. First, we ran fast and hard, then slow and steady. My breathing sped up and grew deep. I felt an overwhelming need for speed, so I resumed the fast and hard pace. Charlie wasn't happy at all, nipping at me more and more and even stepping out in front of me, desperate to get me to stop. But I couldn't stop now. Something was happening. My head was filling up with all kinds of images, some I could control, most I could not.

Images of me over the years began to flash through my mind. In one image, I was yelling at a roomful of my own teammates, threatening them to get their work done on time to meet our deadline. In another, I was cutting off and demeaning one of my direct reports in front of his peers, not caring that he was hurt and embarrassed. In yet another, I was telling a store clerk she was incompetent when she failed for the third time to find the product I was looking for.

Sweat poured down my forehead and soaked every layer of clothing I was wearing. My eyes filled with salty water. As my heart beat faster and blood raced through my veins, I grew concerned about my high blood pressure. But this rush had nothing to do with my workout.

Images continued to flash through my head like the streaks of lightning I had seen on that first night. I saw myself slap a guy across the face for reasons I cannot remember. I recalled passing someone up for a promotion because I didn't want them to be my peer. I remembered telling a competitive peer to stay out of my way or I would make her job very difficult. Recalling these events overwhelmed me, physically and emotionally. I was sweating, my lungs burned, my blood was boiling, and my heart was racing. I cannot explain it. It was as if someone had flipped an electrical switch inside me.

My thoughts were out of control. They were like bullet trains racing in different directions and meeting again at one point: one clear, real, horrific truth.

Suddenly, I was bowled over by a, "No way, OMG!" feeling. I stopped dead in my tracks, right in the middle of the street. I jerked Charlie on his leash as he tried to run forward. I was overcome with embarrassment and horror. I wanted to disappear. I realized what had been shed from my spirit that fateful Monday morning. I could not believe it. Or could I?

Charlie was thrilled we had finally stopped running. He dropped to the ground, enjoying the cold surface beneath him. He stared up at me as I stood frozen. But his happiness didn't last. I picked back up the run, jerking frantically on his leash. When he resisted, I tugged it a few more times, willing him to follow.

The dam of life experiences continued to flood my mind. I was determined to look at each one and figure out what part they had played in the truth with which I was now confronted. It was like watching my life through a 1970's 3-D picture viewer. One-by-one, the images flashed: people I had worked with, hung out with, dated, and even turned my back on. The details were so vivid, it was like they'd happened yesterday.

I replayed entire discussions in my head—fights, confrontations, sweet talks, and episodes I'd provoked. I felt the hurt and attitude I had hurled at others. Every ounce of pain and joy I'd ever felt swept over me. My head was spinning and my heart was pounding. "Oh my God!!" kept replaying in my head, like a broken record.

Had I not been in a public park running in the middle of the street with Charlie, I would have fallen to the ground in fetal position and rocked myself back and forth. I would have yelled, over and over and over again, "*No, no, no! This cannot be happening!*" But it was.

After all this time, I finally got it, and the truth literally knocked me down. For most of my adult life, I had been a complete bitch. Simply put, I had treated people like shit, discarded them if I didn't think were "good enough," and demanded too much from my friends, family, and those I worked with. I lived in a world that was all about me and if someone didn't respond to that, well, let's just say it wasn't pretty. In both my personal and business lives, I had been a bitch! On this chilly November morning, I walked around the park, mortified.

How in the world did this happen? When did I become such a horrible person? Why did I allow myself to become such a bitch? No one deserved that treatment. I am a giving, selfless, nurturing, and loving woman, I thought. Or, was that the woman who was just set free this past week? I couldn't be that curt, spiteful woman that flashed through my 3-D picture viewer. Or could I? Maybe I was and maybe I had shed that ugliness when I walked out of the office building that Monday morning. I prayed to God, as I ran through that park that I had.

Chapter 4

THE MILKMAN'S DAUGHTER

Several weeks later, on a rainy, dark, and cloudy morning, I lay on the couch skimming the pages of the *Atlanta Journal Constitution*. Being vain, I refused to wear my reading glasses, so I had to squint to see the words on the page. What I was able to make out appeared to be a declaration of empowerment. The sentence read,

"*The first step to recovery is admitting you have a problem.*"

I felt as though someone had thrown a glass of cold water in my face. I don't remember if the statement was part of an article or an advertisement. I only know that the words jumped right off the page at me.

The journey I found myself on was one of recovery and discovery. I wanted to recover the sassy, precocious girl I once was. And, I needed to discover why I had created the bitch I had become.

Each morning, I arose early, despite a lack of purpose or structure for the day. Self-discovery and recovery had become my full-time job. I needed to look into my soul and uncover the events—good, bad, happy, and sad—which had brought me to this point in my life. Exhausted from the emotions that continued to overwhelm me, I threw the paper onto the cocktail table, sunk deeper into the couch, and drifted off to sleep.

I dreamed I was in my hometown of Havertown, a suburb of Philadelphia. I was standing on the curb, glancing up at my childhood house. My grandfather had built the small, red brick, three-bedroom carriage house for my parents. It sat amongst the tall oak and pine trees, proudly shielding and protecting our family. I felt warm and safe.

A bunch of kids were racing up and down the hill in the front yard. They would scale the three-foot stone wall that trimmed the base of the yard and jump, landing knee-deep in piles of freshly fallen snow.

It was a gorgeous, sunny afternoon. The sky was clear, and the air brisk. It was a school day, but because a foot of snow had blanketed the streets and highways, school was closed for the day. It was the perfect excuse for us kids to goof off, get out of our parents' way, and play outside for hours in the white, fluffy snow.

My brothers, Chris and Mark, chased their old, rusted wood sled down the driveway. Arms stretched in front of them, they would run behind the sled and try to dive on top of it, like catching the big wave. But as Chris attempted his dive, the metal blades of the sled got stuck; bringing the sled to an abrupt stop and hurling him face-down into the snow. My sisters, Mary, Peggy, and Theresa watched from the top of the driveway and were laughing hysterically. They couldn't wait for their turn to show the boys how it's done. Inside the house, in my parents' bedroom, my mother and Grandma Boas were deep in conversation. I raced inside to join them. In our large family, you didn't get many chances to hang out with your mother and grandma alone.

In the corner of the room, on the chair by the bed, was a white shopping bag that caught my eye. I walked over to sneak a peek, but my grandmother, in her quiet, strict way, glared at me with her piercing eyes and shooed me away. Obediently, I sat quietly on the bed.

As the two women continued talking, my grandmother walked over to the shopping bag, leaned over to open it, and pulled out a beautiful, little girl's dress. I stood up on the bed and slowly walked to the edge where my grandmother stood. With eyes wide, I stared at the dress. It was one of the most beautiful things I had ever seen in my tiny world.

The dress was made of yellow chiffon with hundreds of little eyelet flowers all over it. White lace trimmed the skirt and sleeves. As Grandma held it up, she swung the hanger back and forth to show my mother the way it flowed like a princess' dress. *Please, please,* I prayed. *Please make me the princess.*

Finally, my grandmother said, "I thought Bernadette would look adorable in this." Overjoyed, I began to jump up and down on my parents' bed.

"Yes, she would," my mother agreed. I jumped even higher and giggled louder. I became so excited that I actually peed my pants—and my mother's bed. Not knowing what to do, I stopped jumping and looked up at the two women, afraid that I was now in trouble and wouldn't get my princess dress. Then, I noticed my mother and grandmother straining not to laugh. Unable to hold it, they broke out laughing as they shooed me off of the bed.

Peeing aside, I never felt more loved and special than I did in that moment.

Grandma Boas died a year or so later. I do not remember her very well but I clearly recall her tall, full stature. Her very presence was intimidating. Her stern, cold manner was even more unsettling. She was never the hugs and kisses type, which explained my father's nature. She certainly didn't show her emotions very easily, so the fact that she had bought me such a beautiful dress was a very big deal.

Because she raised my father during the Great Depression, my grandmother was never known for extravagance. She shopped at the local thrift store, as did my father. Whether it was for toys, stuffed animals, or other little gifts, my family frequently visited the thrift store. I never learned for sure that Grandma bought the beautiful, yellow chiffon princess dress for me at the thrift store. But if she had, I wouldn't have cared. I was a princess, according to my two mothers.

Even at three, I knew it was a 'special' dress for a 'special' girl, and that girl was me. Years later, I still remember how special that dress and my grandmother made me feel. The feeling is burned into my memory.

Lying on my couch, I could feel a smile come over my face. I opened my eyes slightly and turned over. Charlie adjusted with me, and we fell back to sleep.

Those early years of feeling 'special' gave way to memories of being 'different'. I was beginning to feel like I didn't belong, neither at school nor at home.

My brothers and sisters and I had just finished a school recital at Manoa Elementary School. My favorite childhood teacher, Mrs. DeCampli, came up to my parents and me and said, "Bernadette, you sang beautifully. I could hear you all the way in the back of the auditorium!" My brothers and sisters broke out in laughter. I jumped in and laughed with them, though I sensed they weren't laughing *with* me but *at* me.

I knew I couldn't sing very well, not nearly as well as my sister, Peggy, or my brother, Jimmy. I often just screamed at the top of my lungs. I so wanted to be heard in those days. The constant noise of my older brothers and sisters often drowned out most of the littler voices, including mine.

Singing was a way for me to be heard and I loved it. I loved to express the words and emotions of a song, and I felt them so clearly, so fully. It always made me feel alive. I loved the thrill of getting up in front of people and entertaining them even more. Getting them to smile, clap, and cheer sent shivers up and down my spine. It was the most exhilarating feeling. I have my parents to thank for that.

My mother and father both had a deep love for music and entertainment, though in completely different ways. My mother had an operatic soprano voice that rang out like an angel each week at Sunday mass and our yearly Christmas concert. As a young girl, she even recorded her own album of various versions of Ave Maria, one of my favorite songs.

She loved classical singers like Andrea Bocelli, Renee Fleming, Jeannette McDonald, and Deana Durbin. Their voices would resonate from the turntable or cassette player each day, as she cleaned or cooked dinner. Over the years, my mother would introduce us to new voices that she followed, such as Charlotte Church, El Divo, Kitty Carlisle, and Enrico Caruso. She said she was searching for God in those voices.

My father, on the other hand, lacked any kind of musical skill or talent. But, he had a passion for all types of music –The Rat Pack of Frank Sinatra,

Sammy Davis, Jr., Dean Martin, Joey Bishop & Peter Lawford, Glenn Miller and Nina Simone, Mel Torme and Rosemary Clooney, Flatt & Scruggs, Benny Goodman, and many more. On many nights, the sound of Elvin Bishop's *Traveling Shoes* would bellow through the rooms of our house. My father would jump out of his overstuffed recliner and break into his chicken dance, making us roar with laughter.

My mother and father went to great lengths to make sure we loved music as much as they did. We took piano, guitar, and trumpet lessons, and even attended old-time fiddler events at Lenape Park, to show off our Irish jig skills. As a result, each and every one of 'the kids,' as my parents called us, developed a similar passion for music. For me, it was acting and improvisational classes, or singing in the choirs and musicals at our church and our school.

We said goodbye to Mrs. DeCampli and raced out of the school auditorium doors. We knew what was coming next. Pulling on my mother's sleeve, my brother Matthew pleaded, "Mommie, are we going for ice cream?"

"Absolutely!" my mother replied, a huge smile on her face.

After each and every recital, my parents would treat us to ice cream sundaes at Barson's restaurant a few miles from the school. It was so exciting for us to go there. We could build our own sundaes, piling them high with everything from jimmies and cherries to peanut pieces and marshmallow sauce, to caramel and any number of fudge toppings that sat on the long counter against the main wall of the restaurant.

We piled into the car, causing it to rock back and forth until we reached the parking lot of Barson's. Before my father could completely stop the car, we jumped out and rushed inside to the waiting line in front of the cash register. My mother and father, panicked, raced in behind us and whispered, "Slow down and be quiet. There are folks trying to enjoy their dinner."

But we didn't care about the old people quietly enjoying their supper; we wanted ice cream and we made sure everyone knew it. Eight of us stood there in line pushing and shoving each other, anxiously awaiting permission to hit the ice cream machines facing us.

The waitress, who knew us from our frequent visits, smiled and said that she would be with us in a minute. For us, a minute standing there in line seemed like forever. To keep ourselves entertained, we continued to push and shove each other. My father glared at us and we quieted down, fast.

As we stood there impatiently waiting our turn, an elderly couple walked up to my parents at the front of the line. Looking over my mother's shoulder and down the line at us, the man asked, "Are all of these children yours?"

Beaming from ear to ear, as he always did when asked this question, my father replied, "Of course they are."

The man walked behind them and over to us. Unsure of what was about to happen, we huddled together, protectively. He looked us up and down and then glanced at me. Without hesitating, he said, "Of course, you must be a friend. How nice it is of them to bring along a friend."

Shocked and confused, I looked up at my father and mother. Inside, I was screaming, *Why is this old man picking me out from the group? Why is he claiming that I am a friend? Why did he think I was not with them, not one of the kids? Does he really think parents of seven would bring along an extra kid that wasn't their own?*

I could feel my face turn beet red. My heart was racing and I felt both mad and very sad. My brothers and sisters were laughing again. I heard my mother say, "Of course, she is one of ours." But the man and woman simply shook their heads, walked away, and left the restaurant. Still stunned, I just stared after them. I couldn't tell if they were impressed or appalled. I wanted to cry, but I simply stood there, silent, confused about why these old people thought that I was not one of my parents' kids.

From the time I was a toddler, I looked different from my brothers and sisters. My blue eyes, blonde, curly hair, and very fair, freckle-less skin stood in stark contrast to the dark hair, brown eyes, and freckled faces of my siblings. When a bunch of us went out together, it became very common for people to look at me and state, *"You must not be one of them."* Or they would ask, *"Are you a Boas, too?"* They would look completely shocked when I said yes.

It didn't help my confidence when my brothers and sisters would burst out laughing, taunt me, and egg them on with comments like, "Yeah, she's the milkman's daughter, or maybe the postman's, we're not sure. She's adopted."

Each time, I would turn red with anger and say, wanting to scream, "No, I am not!"

My parents, who never imagined this jesting was hurtful to me, would brush off my siblings' jeers by saying, "Oh, she is *indeed* one of us. She's the black sheep."

The strangers, with their irritating grin, would respond, "Well, you certainly are different, aren't you?" Each time it happened, I wanted to run and hide.

By the time I was ten years old, the thought that I might have been adopted bothered me. One morning before getting ready for school, I searched the house for my mother. I finally found her in the back room doing laundry. Walking up behind her with tears in my eyes and my head hung low, I tugged on her sleeve and in an unusually serious voice said, "Mom?"

"Yes, sweetie," she replied without turning around.

"Mom, am I really adopted?" I asked, tears streaming down my face.

My mother turned from the pile of clothes she was folding. "Adopted?" What in the world makes you ask that?" she demanded. I could tell from the strained look on her face that she could not believe I was actually asking her that question.

"Because the kids are always saying that I am, or that I'm the milkman's daughter, or the postman's." I continued to cry.

Her strained look turned to sadness. She wrapped her arms around me, pulled me tightly to her chest, and said, "Oh, honey!"

It had suddenly hit her that all of the taunting and what she believed to be just kids' play, was hurting me. The look on her face was piercing. She leaned over, took my face into her soft hands, and with the biggest and warmest smile I had ever seen, said, "Sweetie, of course you aren't adopted. You are all Boas inside and out, like it or not. You're special, and just because you may not look like them now, one day you will see that you are very much like the other kids. "

I threw my arms around her stomach, pulling myself in tightly against her for one of her great hugs, and started to cry. I heard a whimper or two from her as well, though I couldn't bring myself to look up at her. All I knew was that I had that 'special' feeling again. *She called me 'special' and not 'different'.* I was overcome with happiness.

I shifted again and Charlie rolled over and on top of me. His eighty pounds nearly smothered me, but I was too tired to care. I drifted off again into dreamland.

I was down in the basement where 'the kids', our cousins, and I were playing with my grandfather's train set, dancing across the black and white checkered floor, and playing hide-and-seek. My mother called for us to come up and join the family in the living room.

Bored and not wanting to sit on the floor, the only place to sit once the older kids took the chairs and sofa, I excused myself and went to roam my grandparent's three-story row home. In all the times we visited, I rarely spent time on the second or third floors. For some reason, on this day, I wanted to learn more about the home where my mother grew up. I envisioned her as a child running and yelling through the halls, jumping on her parents' bed, and fighting with her old brother, Jim and younger sisters, Peggy and Eileen. The idea of my mother being a playful, mischievous girl excited me.

Starting in the back of the house where my grandparents' room was, I began sneaking around each of the rooms. From the hallway, I could smell the scent of smoke from my grandfather's pipe which lingered on the velvet chairs and window curtains in each of the rooms.

The rooms were dark, even with the lights on, so I had to get close up to anything I wanted to see in my grandparents' room. There was a small, porcelain doll lying against the bed pillows. Family photographs lined the walls and dressers. There were photos of Grand Mom and Grand Pop, as well as our Uncle Phonce, Uncle Jimmy, Sister Rose, and my Godfather, Uncle Bill.

I made my way back down the hallway to the bedroom my mother had shared with her younger sister, my Aunt Peggy. It sat at the top of the stairs just like the bedroom I shared with my little sister, Patricia.

I walked slowly around my mother's small room, wanting to touch everything. I imagined her and Aunt Peggy whispering under the bedcovers late at night, or playing dress up at the vanity, just like Patricia and I did. Sitting on the small bed, I wondered what my mother was like as a young girl and then as a teenager. Did she hang out with friends, listen to music, play and giggle with her little sisters, try on her mother's dresses and jewelry, or pretend to be getting married, just like we did?

I glanced around the room one last time and noticed a framed photo on the vanity against the window. I had never noticed it before. I walked over and picked it up. Even though it was daylight, the room was so dark I could hardly see the photo. I walked out to the hallway to get a better look.

The photo was actually a hand painting of two young girls, one about age seven or eight and the other, about four. They were adorable.

Wow, I thought. *That's Mary. How could it be?* Then, it hit me. The older girl in the photo was actually my mother when she was about eight years old. The resemblance between her and my sister, Mary, was uncanny.

The other young girl in the photo, I figured, was my Aunt Peggy. But it didn't really look like her. The image looked more like me when I was four; the blue eyes, blonde, wavy hair, and freckle-less, fair skin. Suddenly, it all made sense. The girl in the photo was my Aunty Peggy. *She looked just like me!*

God, I thought, *I have finally found my connection, the link to the Boas kids*. It didn't come from my mother or my father. My appearance, the thing that made so many people call me out as 'different', was actually like that of my lovely and sweet Aunt Peggy, my mother's younger sister. *Why hadn't I ever considered that?* All these years, I had questioned whether I belonged to this family when all this time, I was just an Aunt away, a Clearkin (my mother's maiden name) away. I was indeed one of the Boas kids. I finally felt as if I belonged. That meant everything to me.

I danced around the hallway with such excitement that Anne Marie and Theresa ran upstairs to see what was going on. I knew if I said anything to either of them or the others they would laugh at me again, so I kept it to myself. I placed the painting back onto my mother's childhood dresser and went back downstairs. I was tempted to hide the painting under my shirt so I could take a part of me home, but I didn't; at least, not that day.

A decade later, after both my grandparents had passed away, I claimed it as my own. My mother had inherited it. During a visit to my parents' house in Philadelphia, I saw the painting sitting on a dresser in one of the empty bedrooms. Truly believing that painting should be mine, I packed it in my travel bag and took it home. Many years later, on a visit to my home in Florida, my mother saw it proudly displayed on my living room console. She smiled gently and said, "I am glad you have it, Sweetie". She had always known I had it and understood the significance of that painting, how 'special' it was to me.

It turned out my mother was right all along. When I reached my early twenties, I began to notice the physical traits of my brothers and sisters in my own reflection in the mirror. It was the shape of my eyes, my thin upper lip, the stomach "pooch," which all the Boas girls have. And then, there was my voice, deep and raspy like my sister, Peggy's. I was all Boas...and damn proud of it!

Still, being 'different' ruled my psyche for a very long time. Even though I'd finally recognized the physical link to my siblings, I still felt like an outsider. For me, those days of feeling 'different' influenced a great deal of who I would become and played an even bigger role as I transformed myself from beloved to bitch, and from bitch back to beloved.

Chapter 5

THE KIDS

"Bernadette, do it again, do it again!" squealed the kids sitting in a circle on the ground of Manoa Elementary School.

"And go as fast as you can!"

Rolling my eyes at having to do this for the hundredth time, I took a deep breath and blurted out as fast as my mouth would move, "Chris, Mark, Mary, Peggy, Theresa, Anne Marie, Matthew, Bernadette, Michael, Jimmy, Patricia, and Britt!"

"Wow, four seconds!" Eddie cheered.

The kids giggled as I turned red with embarrassment. Rolling my eyes again, I replied, "It's no big deal".

It was a big deal. I was very proud of my oversized family. I also had fun with those constant requests to rattle off all of our names. As a child, I was often confused as to why so many other kids and even adults found it fascinating that we had such a large family. *Didn't everyone have at least twelve kids in their family?* I wondered. My next door neighbors had thirteen; what was so odd about that? In our predominately Irish Catholic parish and neighborhood, it was common for families to have five or more kids. Some, like ours, the Welde's, McCarrey's, and McKee's, had eleven or twelve.

But to the kids on the playground, we were oddballs. They would shoot off questions at me, trying to imagine what it must be like to live under the same roof with all of those kids.

"How big is your house?"

"Where do you all sleep?"

"How do your parents feed all of you?"

"Do you have to share your toys?"

"Do you even get toys?"

"What is Christmas like?"

"It must be awesome!" they'd say. It *was* awesome.

Everyone we ran into had similar reactions. When my parents would pile us into the car to take us out, folks would stare, stunned to see us walk single-file into church or the clothes store, or restaurants. Most of the time, the cashiers or store clerks would walk away, praying we wouldn't pull our five or six shopping carts into their lane. Waitresses avoided us, hoping we would find another section of the restaurant, so they wouldn't have to deal with a dozen screaming and hyper kids. At church, we took up a whole pew, which didn't thrill many of the parishioners. They were bothered by it, but I enjoyed the attention we received. I loved standing out.

Even today, people ask questions that always make me laugh.

"Are you Catholic?"

"You must be Irish, right?"

"Where are you from?" It's like I'm from some strange place that breeds families with ten or more children.

When people ask if we are Catholic or Irish, I often play with them. With a stone cold expression, I'll turn to them and say, "No, we're Jewish!" They wait a second or two to see if I'm serious, then a look of complete shock comes over their face. Their eyes get wide and their mouths hang open. They're never sure what to say. After all, I am fair-skinned and blue-eyed. I'll let them sweat for ten seconds or so, and then I'll chuckle and say, "Only kidding! Of course, we're Irish and Catholic!" Immediately, they exhale, relieved. I always get a kick out of that.

I have heard all the comments, snickers, and jokes. In high school, even nuns and priests would have a field day at our expense. They would joke, in front of the entire class, "Boy, your father didn't bowl much, did he?" The class would burst into laughter and I would once again turn beet red, completely disgusted. After all, they were nuns and priests!

It was no surprise to anyone that my parents would have a large family. After all, both of them were devout Catholics, did not believe in birth control, and had complete faith in God's plan—oh, and the rhythm method! It became obvious to many people in our close, Irish Catholic parish that God was a lot more dependable than the rhythm method.

Comments and jokes aside, being one of the twelve 'Boas Kids' was an experience in itself. We had a complete baseball, basketball, or flag football team. We had a built-in circle of friends and ready-made slumber parties. We even had our own in-house clothing store; unfortunately, the goods were mostly hand-me-downs. We had our own used sports equipment and musical instrument stores, as well. And we always had an instant party—and we all knew how to party!

Best of all, we had our own group of tutors, teachers, coaches, and advisors to help solve any personal, educational, or professional dilemma we might have. That has always been the most important part of all. My eleven brothers and sisters, each in his or her way, became the greatest influences in my life. They taught me a great deal about 'the boys' club', teamwork, competition, delegation, negotiation, and facilitation. We were a small business, or maybe more like a small country, made up of very different political, cultural, and business views. There were so many personalities and examples to learn from. It was the perfect training ground for life in corporate America.

From my earliest memory, my brothers and sisters and I were always close, emotionally and physically. The twelve of us were born within a fifteen-year span. This caused my oldest brother, Chris, to quip that he never knew my mother without a belly.

That three-bedroom brick house on Oak Way forced us all to learn to live closely with, practically on top of, one another. Three sets of bunk beds filled two of the bedrooms that the six girls and six boys shared. Our living room was so small the twelve of us completely covered the floor when we watched TV. The narrow dining room could barely hold the long table around which we would squeeze to enjoy evening supper.

Our expansive back yard was the one place that gave us room to spread our wings and our energy. The patio was so large that my father turned it into an ice skating rink in the winter and a pool deck in the summer. We had a sandbox large enough for several of us to play in at one time, and a dense area of trees we used as our own private island. It served as an escape for me and most of my siblings, but the small house was the glue that held us together.

Then, one day out of the blue, my father announced that we would be moving from our small brick house. *Moving?* I thought. *I love this house.* At the top of his lungs, so those of us in the backyard or on the second floor could hear, he bellowed, "Let's go! Everyone get your shoes on, we're going for a walk!"

All twelve of us gathered in the living room.

"Okay, everybody hold hands!" my mother directed as we made our way out of the house and up Oak Way toward Manoa Road. My father led the way while my mother walked at the back holding Britt in her arms. A few of the older kids and I held the tiny hands of Patricia, Jimmy, and Michael, as we all marched single-file on Eagle Road. As we passed our grade school playing field, we got excited, thinking we were going to go play ball or maybe chase in the large baseball field.

When we reached the end of the field, my father stopped in his tracks, causing all of us to bump into one another. A chain reaction of, "Hey, watch it, get off of me!" rang out.

My mother, still holding Britt, yelled, "Quiet down now!"

My father then turned toward a large white stone house with the green shutters and two chimney stacks, proudly announcing, "Kids, this is our new home!"

For a second, we all stood there, silently staring at the biggest house we had ever seen. Then, like wildfire, we all took off for the front steps, screaming, "Yippee!" Chris threw open the screened front door and slammed it hard against the foyer wall.

"Be careful!" my dad yelled. None of us heard him.

Still squealing with delight, most of the kids ran through the rooms on the first floor. There was a musty library that would become our den and dining room, a living room with a stone fireplace, a back porch, a huge backyard, a laundry room, and a small kitchen that would never hold all fourteen of us at one time.

Peggy, Mary, and the rest of the girls ran up to the second floor to check out the bedrooms, quickly claiming our favorite one for ourselves. *Yeeeeeee!* I thought. *Finally, we won't all have to share a single room.* Yes, I would have a roommate, my youngest sister, Patricia, but I wouldn't have five of them.

Anne Marie and Matthew found the intercoms that hung on the walls in the hallways. "Hello, anyone there?'" Matthew called.

"Hello down there," a voice from the third floor yelled back. *Cool,* I thought. *Space, freedom, and peace. This house is huge!* It was huge, to this group of six to ten year-olds.

We were never at a loss for friends. Even when we didn't have our own from school, the swim club, or the playground, we always had each other. You don't go without friends and fun when you have a ready-made sports team for a family. We now had a basketball court, a large field across the street, and a backyard that would make for some great chases. I would laugh with my friends and tell them to come over to our house on any Saturday night and check out the kids' wrestling matches. "They're a blast," I told them.

Wrestling matches were our Saturday night entertainment. When we would get restless or bored, we would turn our living room or bedrooms into a ring and wrestle or have pillow fights. Most of the time, it was the boys tackling the girls. They would hold us down while smothering us with pillows. Kicking, screaming, and laughing, the girls would end up kicking the boys where it hurt to get free, or tickle them so hard, they'd pee their pants. This would go on for hours or until our mother or father yelled for us to stop.

Sometimes, seven or eight of us would find our way to my parents' room and arrange ourselves on their king size bed, head to toe, until we all could fit. Then, we would stroke the arm of the one next to us, gently running the tips of our fingers up and down each other's arms. In a matter of minutes, peaceful sighs would fill the room. If Matthew or one of the boys didn't disrupt the quiet with their antics, the room would grow quiet and still and most of us would fall asleep. Now that was a sleep remedy!

Moving into that huge house didn't stop us from living and loving in close proximity to one another. As the years went on, many of us turned out to be best friends, and to this day, all twelve of us get together quite regularly to break open a beer or two and celebrate life.

Many times over the years I have wondered whether our family is too good to be true. And then I decide, absolutely not.

Like all families, we had personality clashes, disagreements with our parents, and childhood wounds. Compared to the tragedies and hardships so many other families have to deal with, our issues seemed trivial. In fact, every night when I lay my head on my pillow, I thank God for the family He blessed me with. We are quite the dozen.

Chris and Mark, the two oldest boys, are like the comic strip characters, Mutt and Jeff. They went to school together, played sports, fly fished, and got into trouble together. They were the second and third fathers we never asked for but they thought we needed.

Mary and Peggy, eleven months apart, couldn't be more different from one another. They spent their entire childhood at the same schools, at the same country club pool, and around the same neighborhood, but their many differences sent them into completely different directions. Mary, or "Duchess," as my father called her, is the academic, flower child, and activist. Many called her the Marsha Brady of the family. Peggy, more like Jan Brady, is the artistic creative with street smarts that no book could teach. She was drawn to music, the stage, and the road to promote her CD, *Pop Goes the Weasel*. Mary went off to Alabama and California in search of independence and herself. Mary and Peggy couldn't be more different and yet their love/hate relationship has glued them together in so many ways.

Theresa and Anne Marie had a friendship everyone envied. They went to school together, hung out with each other's friends, and were bound at the hip from childhood through adulthood. They loved sharing a bedroom. It drove Patricia and me crazy when they forced us to switch rooms each summer. They wanted to find out which room was better, so they could claim it for their own.

Michael and Jim were characters, who pretended not to like each other when around their friends, yet were inseparable when at home. Both talented athletes and party animals, they kept my parents on their toes. They caddied, played golf together, and were on the same soccer team. They respected each other's talents and reveled in the other's antics.

Patricia and Britt, the two youngest, were never considered the babies of the family, but they certainly were *my babies*. I watched after them as if they were my own and developed a love for them that was different from the love I had for my other brothers and sisters. Not more or less, just different. I adore them both.

As the youngest, they had the chance to carefully observe their ten siblings and decide what and who they wanted to emulate. They are both kind and gentle and have athletic abilities the rest of us envy.

Matthew and I were the stereotypical middle children. We never fit with any one sibling and had to find our own way. Matthew spent most of his youth rebelling against anything and everything my parents, his teachers, or his counselors advised and created quite the uproar in the house. He made the rest of us look like angels, and tested the limits of my parents' philosophy, "what we don't know won't hurt us". Today, Matthew is one of the most respected men in our home town.

As for me, when I wasn't being my usual, smart aleck self, I sought every possible way to get attention—from anyone. Whether it was the school choir, church plays, or the sports field, I fought to be the best, the loudest, and the fastest. I'd do anything to get the award, the cheers, or the attention. Most times, it just got me into trouble.

I revered my sister Peggy's singing and acting talent. I would sit, riveted, when she practiced her lines for *Funny Girl*, when she had the lead role of *Fanny Brice*. While helping her rehearse, I would act out the part, imagining myself on the stage belting out *Don't Rain on my Parade* and receiving *a* standing ovation. But it wasn't me. It was Peggy, and every time she sang the crowd would stand. It was awesome.

I trailed after my big sisters, Theresa and Anne Marie. Theresa was an amazing athlete. You name it—field hockey, swimming, or softball, she was the MVP, and I wanted to be just like her. Anne Marie was fun. She loved to laugh, flirt, and be silly. It was contagious and I often followed her just to be part of it.

I'm not sure what any of them would say about me and what influence, if any, I had on their lives, but they certainly influenced mine. Over the years, many of us moved away from Philadelphia to find our own lives, but we never really separated from one another. We simply took the time and distance to discover who and what we were away from the noise of the crowded house.

Eventually, all of them found their way home, back to Philadelphia, and the friends who will always have their back.

I am the only one who lives away from home. My excuse has always been that after eighteen years of noise and limited space, I needed eighteen years of peace and space to spread my wings. Over the last ten years, I have longed for the noise and space constraints, but not necessarily for Philadelphia.

Fortunately, we still regularly come together like we did when we were kids. There have been ten weddings and twenty-two nieces and nephews. Our friendship with each other has deepened and new relationships have been born. My six brothers, their sons, and their friends' sons nurture their bond each spring as they continue my father's fifty-year tradition of attending Jungle Cock, a fly fishing camp in Maryland. For three days and two nights, they fish, camp, cook-out, and laugh together. And every Mother's Day week, all of the girls pile into minivans or sports cars and take my mother on our own version of Jungle Cock; we call it Jungle Hen. For eight days, we take off for the beaches of Ocean City, New Jersey to do nothing but eat, drink, and laugh.

I'm not sure how we've managed to continually nurture, build, and grow our relationships with one another despite distance or differences, but we do. For me to say that any of my brothers or sisters influenced the bitch that I became would be unfair to them. No matter what they might have thought of me during those greedy, ego-centered years, they never once judged me. They may not have liked me at times; they may have even despised me, but they loved me no matter what.

Chapter 6

MY ROCK

My mother ran from the kitchen and up the flight of stairs to the second floor yelling, "Come on, catch me if you can!" When she reached the top of the stairs, she squatted down behind the banister and waited. Anne Marie, Theresa, and I raced as fast as we could after her, almost falling over each other. As we reached the top step and turned the corner, my mother jumped out and screamed, "Gotcha!" She pulled the three of us close and tickled us. I fell to the ground laughing so hard I almost peed myself. She had a way of doing that to us.

Born Mary Ann Clearkin to a wealthy Philadelphia couple, my mother was raised with a silver spoon in her mouth. Growing up in fancy dresses and patent leather shoes, and educated at private schools—with Princess Grace, no less—my mother was the epitome of high society.

As a child, I spent many hours in her room twirling around in her long raccoon or mink coat, dressing up in her pearls and floor-length gowns or dresses, and wearing her Hermes scarves, hats, and pocketbooks. The scent of powdery perfume clung to the items that hung in her closet. I would lie on her bed and picture her as a teenage girl at a fancy dance or strolling along the Wildwood Boardwalk arm in arm with one of her many beaus. She was a beautiful woman.

Her high-society upbringing made her into a soft-spoken, classy, God-fearing woman. And did I mention that she was beautiful? Her petite frame, dark, wavy hair, and piercing blue eyes, set her apart from many of the girls she grew up with.

My mother had a bottomless well of love for her family and other people in her life. She did not marry into the wealthy Philadelphia family as her parents had hoped. She did fall in love and marry a man who gave her everything she truly wanted—children, family, love, and security—for more than fifty years.

Although she left her high-society lifestyle when she married my father, my mother never wanted for anything. All she ever wanted was to create the most loving home for her children. For her, that meant a warm bed, hot meals, loving hugs, and rooms filled with laughter.

She had absolutely no attachment to money. In fact, she gave any money she received to her children, including her inheritance and the allowance my father gave her. As long as I can remember, she never asked for anything. When I found myself in a tight spot as an adult, she gave me everything she had.

In 1999, I called my sister, Peggy, to tell her about some credit card debt I had and told her I needed a quick fix. I didn't expect Peggy to bail me out, because she wasn't exactly rolling in dough. But she always had good ideas for this kind of thing, and I needed to talk to someone.

The last thing I expected was for her to tell anyone about my predicament. When the phone rang and I heard my mother's voice, telling me she wanted to come for a visit, I nearly broke down in tears. Peggy had spoken to my mother, and as usual, she would do whatever she could to take care of one of her children. But I wasn't a child anymore. I didn't want my mother to come to my rescue, especially financially. I made more than enough money to pay off this debt. It would just take too long and cost too much in interest. I needed a short-term solution. My mother decided she was it.

A day into her visit, we were sitting in my living room talking about my latest break up. As tears streamed down my face, my mother reached out and took my hand. Her soft, cool hands stroked mine and I was five years old again. I laid my head on her chest and wrapped my arms around her. As mothers always do, Mom knew my tears were not just about the breakup. In her soft voice, she gently said, "And don't worry yourself over that credit card issue. I have it with me."

I wiped my eyes, looked into hers, and leaned my head back into her chest. "I love you, Mom," I whispered hoarsely.

"I love you too, Sweetie," she said. It is that selfless love that inspires every one of her children to revere her. She radiates such inner strength, unflinching faith, and pure love that you feel as if you're in an angel's presence.

Don't be fooled by her 5'3" frame. She's a fighter who would fight to the death for her family. Anyone who ever tried to cross my mother's children regretted it. Take it from Timmy, the neighborhood bully who lived down the street.

By the age of fifteen, Timmy had been in and out of juvenile detention—and even jail—for everything from fighting and vandalism to petty theft. Local cops said he had a rap sheet so long; he'd be put away if he ever crossed the line into something more serious. He wasn't only well-known by the cops; his victims' parents knew him and his family all too well. Timmy took great pride in knocking boys down, and his parents weren't much better.

Timmy's parents allowed him to rule the neighborhood with his fists, something which sadly, he learned at home. It was no secret that there was frequent domestic abuse inside their home.

Timmy and my brother, Matthew, were the same age and attended the same school. That's where the trouble started. Matthew wouldn't back down to Timmy, so the bully kept coming after him.

Matthew, a troublemaker himself, enjoyed egging Timmy on, trying to provoke him into a fight. Other times, Matthew would intervene when Timmy was beating on another kid. Whatever the case, Matthew would often return home with a bloody nose and lip. My mother grew more upset each time he did.

"You are not to interfere here, Mary," my father would say to her. "He has to fight his own battles."

"To what point, Fred?" she'd ask.

That point came early one evening when Matthew ran into the house yelling for my mother. His t-shirt was ripped and splattered with blood and his nose bled down his face. "That's it!" my mother declared. She grabbed Matthew by the arm, stormed out the back door and down the steps straight to Timmy's house, just a few blocks away.

With four or five of us scurrying behind her, my mother stormed up the driveway to the house. She knocked on the door and yelled for Timmy to come out. Like a caged animal, she paced back and forth. Matthew stood beside my mother. You could tell from his stance—head cocked back, chest out—that he was proud she was standing up for him.

Timmy came to the door with his mother close behind. He threw open the screen and with a scowl across his face, yelled, "He started it!" pointing at Matthew.

I held Britt and Patricia's hands as we stood about thirty feet away on the other side of the street. I had never seen my mother so full of rage. She had had it with this bully beating on her kid. It didn't matter whether he had provoked it or not. Matthew caused her plenty of stress and frustration, but this kid beating up on him on a regular basis was another story. My mother wasn't going to stand for it.

Timmy walked up to my mother with an arrogant swagger, tossed Matthew an evil glare and got right in my mother's face. *Who knows what this delinquent is capable of?* I thought. His mother stood behind him, silently swaying back and forth, probably drunk.

My mother grabbed Timmy by the shirt collar, threw back her fist, and punched him square in the face. He fell back a foot or two. Then, she leaned to about an inch from Timmy's face and said, "How does that feel?" She finished with a stern warning, "You touch my son one more time and I will show you what my fist really feels like."

Woahhhhh, I thought, watching in disbelief. *Mom just knocked the devil out of Timmy. Go Mom!* Timmy was fifteen; he could have thrown one punch at her and knocked her to the ground. But she stood in front of him firm and strong. Timmy wasn't about to touch her, and as it turned out, he never touched Matthew again.

I don't know where my mother finds her inner strength; she would say it's from her children. I would have to say God. She is truly a saint. Throughout my life, I have admired her unconditional loyalty and unabashed faith in us. I will never forget when my oldest brother, Chris, confided he was getting a divorce.

Because my mother is a devout Catholic, I figured this would seriously test every ounce of her faith. My parents did not believe in divorce, which they had made clear to us throughout our lives. Yet, here was their eldest son getting divorced. My parents called a family meeting at my brother's place to discuss it. I flew in from Atlanta. I expected to hear them preach about the sanctity of marriage and give us the Catholic guilt trip about divorce. When we were all together, my mother simply took Chris' hand and said, "Honey, you deserve to be happy. If divorcing her will make you happy, you have to do it."

I was flabbergasted. Sitting on the floor at her feet, I looked up at my mother and in my usual, short-tempered way, said, "What? Are you kidding? You don't believe in divorce. It's against our religion!"

The entire room fell silent. I heard one of my siblings say, "Oh, here she goes," as the whole room braced for one of my tirades.

In her calm, sweet manner, my mother looked down at me and said, "You're right; but this is my son. If divorce is what he wants, then that is what he needs to get." We all were stunned. *Wow, she will even change her own beliefs for the happiness of one of her children*, I thought. I pictured her on her knees or lying in bed that night praying for forgiveness.

I have often tried to emulate my mother's relentless passion and loyalty for the people I love, even when I wasn't being the most loving daughter myself. Take, for instance, the very first time I lied to her.

It was Saturday, January 24, just a few days before my fourteenth birthday. Until that day, my mother had never been concerned that I was a year or two younger than other kids in my class. Then I met Joyce in second period History. We became instant best friends.

By ninth-grade standards, Joyce was cool, not because she was the most popular or a cheerleader or the funniest or nicest girl at school. Joyce's cool was the trouble-making cool; the cool the nerds in the corner of the lunch room were scared of and the jocks turned a nose to. She was the cool that smoked, cursed, took risks and dared authority, while everyone else played it safe. Joyce was the cool that every good girl wanted to be, at least once. She was short and thin, with wedge-cut hair like the legendary ice skater, Dorothy Hamill. Her eyes were often thick with eye liner and mascara. She wore vampy, red lipstick like no teenager should. Joyce was the consummate smart-ass bad girl, like "Rizzo," in the movie, *Grease*. She was the female version of a thug in a leather jacket, white t-shirt with a box of cigarettes in the sleeve, and motorcycle. Most of the ninth-grade girls were envious and scared of her. Joyce was the cool I definitely wanted to be in ninth grade, taking chances without getting caught.

Her life was the polar opposite of mine. Joyce came from a broken home. She wore it on her face, in her walk, and attitude toward life. She lived with her mother and never saw her father. Joyce was trouble with a capital T! I knew it and my mother knew it. We didn't know she'd be the reason I'd betray my mother's trust for the first time.

Joyce wanted me to spend the day with her in Atlantic City to celebrate my birthday. "*Atlantic City*! Why *Atlantic City*?" I asked.

"I wanna see Fuzzy," she replied. Fuzzy was her boyfriend, her much older boyfriend. Her mother had forbidden her to see him. He was twenty-four and she was fifteen. "I'm almost sixteen," she would say to justify the relationship.

"We don't even drive, Joyce!" I protested.

"Fuzzy will pick us up and drop us off tonight. All you have to do is tell your mother you're spending the day with me. I'll tell mine I'm spending the day at your house."

"There is no way my mother would ever approve," I tried to explain.

"Then don't ask!" Joyce retorted.

That was not about to happen. Of course, when I asked my mother she said, "Absolutely not! You are way too young to be running off with friends to Atlantic City, birthday or no birthday," she said sternly. It didn't help that it had been snowing for days and the cold temperatures had caused the roads to ice over.

I told Joyce what my mother said. She convinced me to lie to her. "Come on, you deserve this. It's your fourteenth birthday!"

At noon that Saturday, I jumped into the back seat of Fuzzy's Lincoln with Joyce. I didn't care about the consequences; this would be an adventure and a day I would never forget. Fuzzy took off down the street, made a left onto Eagle Road, and passed my house on the left as we headed for the highway.

Ninety minutes later, we were in Atlantic City. There, we met up with Fuzzy's roommate, John, another twenty-something who reeked of trouble. We stopped at a bar and made our way back to their apartment, where we drank beer and smoked pot. I began to pray that I would get back home safe.

Don't get me wrong. I had a blast hanging out with college guys. What I feared was returning home to find that my mother had learned of my betrayal. For the first time in my life, I had lied to her. The idea of lying to her was punishment enough. She didn't deserve it and the Catholic guilt was killing me. *She taught me better than this*, I thought. *I don't lie and deceive people I love.* Though my parents lived by the credo, *"What we don't know won't hurt us"*, *I* was beginning to sense that on this night, they would know and be hurt.

At around nine o'clock p.m., Fuzzy's car drove down Eagle Road and pulled up to our house. I was in the back seat with John staring straight ahead, nervous about reaching my house. As the car approached and pulled up along the curb, I could make out the outline of my mother standing in the front foyer. My heart sank and I felt sick to my stomach.

Without saying a word to Joyce, John, or Fuzzy, I jumped out of the car and walked slowly toward the front door, my head hung low. My hands shook as I reached for the door knob. I felt like vomiting. I pulled the door open and stumbled inside. My mother stood there, glaring at me. Her eyes were dark and swollen. I could tell she had been crying. *Oh my God*, I thought. "Get up to your room, and don't stop until you get there!" was all she said.

I walked through the foyer and went straight up the stairs to my room. Several of my brothers and sisters and my Aunt Leona were sitting in the living room. Catching a glimpse of myself in the mirror, I saw that John had left a couple of hickies on my neck. My heart began to race.

When I heard my mother climbing the stairs, I jumped onto my bed, grabbed a pillow to my chest to cover up my neck, and waited. When she opened the door, I could see that she was more hurt and scared than she was angry; more disappointed than mad. That was even worse. I would much rather have her be pissed than disappointed in me.

"How could you lie to me, Bernadette?" she asked. I told you 'no' because it was too dangerous to drive that far, plus I had no idea who you were going with! You're only thirteen, for God sake!" *Almost fourteen,* I wanted to yell, but didn't.

The anguish on her face made me break down and tell her the whole story. I apologized for hurting and disappointing her, though I never apologized for drinking, smoking, or the hickies on my neck. I couldn't even promise it would never happen again. After all, I was in high school and I knew myself better. I couldn't make false promises or lie to her again. I did tell her I would never see John again.

"Absolutely not!" she agreed. "Joyce either!" She added. That stung, because Joyce was dangerously fun and I wasn't done having fun, just lying. I decided I'd work off of her credo, what she didn't know wouldn't hurt her. I just needed to do a better job making sure she didn't find out.

I wish the story ended there but it didn't, and my mother would prove once again how strong and loyal she is to her children.

John called a few days later to find out when we could get together again.

"I can't see you again, John."

Defiant, he yelled, "You can't break up with me!"

I snapped, "We weren't going out John, and my mother and father won't allow me to see you!"

He yelled, "We'll see about that!" and slammed down the phone. I was scared. *What did he mean? What was he going to do?* I got a sickening feeling in my stomach and was relieved that my mother forbade me to see him again.

Over the next couple of weeks, John began to stalk me, and then my father. Night after night, the phone would ring and each time, I'd begin to tremble. John would warn whoever answered the phone that he was going to get me. I locked myself in my room for days at a time, fearful that if I left the house he would do something. On one call, he threatened, "I watch your father leave every morning in his white Valore. You better hope he gets home tonight." I hung up the phone, crying and trembling, wondering how he knew what kind of car my father drove.

The calls came to an abrupt stop one evening when my father yelled out from behind me, "Keep him on a couple more minutes so the cops can tape it."

Hearing that, John screamed, "Tell your father that I know he isn't taping this!" He slammed down the phone and never called again.

A month or so later, while watching my younger sister, Patricia, at the local school fair, someone whispered, "So Bernadette, any strange calls lately?" I turned around to see John behind me with a smart-ass grin on his face. My two brothers, who were standing close by, ran over and jumped on him. One of them raced to get my mother, who was in the gym working at one of the casino tables.

Within minutes, my mother yanked John from behind, spun him toward her, and warned, "You stay away from my daughter and my family, or you will have all of us to deal with." John ran as fast as he could from the school grounds and us.

After making sure I was okay, she smiled and went back to the poker table she was manning. I will never forget my mother's strength and loyalty.

How do you repay a woman who sacrificed her entire life for you, put your happiness in front of hers, and never asked you for anything? It wasn't until I was in my forties that I could, and her giggle of excitement made it all worthwhile.

In the summer of 2007, I was consumed with work, climbing the corporate ladder, and my beautiful new home in an affluent Atlanta neighborhood. It was my dream home, the reward for my hard work and ambition. It was one of my many material obsessions in those days. I gave little value to the non-materialistic things that make up a truly happy life, the things my mother possessed that I told her weren't important to me. At the time, it was the truth.

I was sitting in my home office, pounding away on my laptop. I was finalizing a major presentation I had with the leadership team the next day, when the phone rang. I answered and was shocked to hear her voice.

"Hi, Sweetie," she said.

"Hey, Mom," I said. "Is everything okay?"

"Yes, everything is fine. I just have a favor to ask."

"Anything," I replied, and then swallowed hard and prayed the favor wouldn't prevent me from finishing my work and meeting my tight deadlines. At that moment, I didn't have time for 'anything'.

Excitedly, she explained that our family church was taking a four-day bus trip to Cape Cod and she really wanted to go. "I need someone to accompany me," she said.

At eighty years young, my mother's spirit was spry, but her body was not. She had trouble walking and often needed a wheelchair and assistance to get around.

"Cape Cod? What dates?" I asked, praying for dates months away, far away from the urgency of my work, house renovations, and social life.

"We would leave from Sacred Heart on Monday, July 16 and return on Friday morning, July 20," she said.

"July? For a full week?" I asked, incredulously.

"I understand if you can't, honey. I know how busy you are," she remarked. I felt horrible that she heard the hesitation and uncertainty in my voice. My heart sank.

"Knowing how good a time you had with Dad in Paris, I thought you would really enjoy this," she said.

Back in 2000, my father asked me to accompany him on a trip to Paris. I didn't hesitate, knowing that it would be one of those rare trips you get to take with a parent. Growing up with eleven brothers and sisters, none of us ever had that opportunity. Not only did I have it with my father, but this was a chance to have it with my mother.

Here it was, the first time she asked me for anything. Asking me to do the same thing I did for my father. Yet, I was allowing my selfishness to make her feel like an inconvenience. *Damn*, I thought. *She doesn't deserve me saying no to her. She doesn't deserve me making her feel she's not worthy of my time and sacrifice. How in the world do you say no to a woman who has given you everything, and more importantly, never asked for a thing in return?* I was not going to let this opportunity slip by.

"Of course I'll go with you, Mom," I said, forcing excitement into my voice.

"Yippee!" she squealed. I laughed. I had never heard my mother squeal before. I pictured her jumping out of her big red recliner in the corner of her living room, throwing up her arms, exhilarated.

"I'm so excited," she went on.

"I am too, Mom," I agreed.

We went over some travel details, working out exactly when I would need to arrive and when I would fly back out. Her excitement was evident in every inflection of her voice and her giggle. When I hung up the phone, I felt nauseous and quickly dismissed it. *My mother deserved this trip. I owe it to her,* I thought.

It turned out to be a fabulous week, and the joy she felt in spending time with her parish friends and me was glorious. Every day I spend time with her, I learn more about her and myself. Whether I understood the lessons at the time, her influence continues to impact me as a woman.

My mother didn't teach us the traditional mother-daughter things like sewing, cooking, or tending to a husband. She knew times were different than when she was young. Teaching us how to sew when ready-to-wear was the norm held little value. Teaching us to tend to a husband full-time when all of her daughters were working women was pointless. And teaching us to cook when she only knew how to cook for fourteen… well, that was just plain funny. She knew the times were changing and amazingly, she changed with them.

She taught the boys what a loving woman, mother, and wife should be by her example. Each of them prayed they would find a woman like her.

If my mother taught me anything over the years, it was to put life, love, and family first. To appreciate the smallest things in life, the intangible things, the things that really matter. It took me too long to learn those lessons. I would sacrifice a full and happy life for many years before I would eventually learn. In the meantime, whenever I need to reconnect with my inner child, I call my mother to hear her say, "Hi, Sweetie."

Chapter 7

MY HERO

"**C**lose your eyes tight," my father commanded from the far end of the dining table, where all fourteen of us were seated for evening supper. "Keep them shut now, and don't open them until I say so."

When my father gave us a command, we listened and obeyed. There was no disrespecting him or my mother, not under his roof. All twelve of us sat straight up in our chairs, shoulders back and chests out, whenever we sat with him. This time, though, our eyes were glued shut and none of us made a peep. We didn't dare.

"Okay. Now focus on the salt and pepper shakers that are under my hat," he said. His beige, wool fedora sat on the table in front of him. Under it, he had placed the crystal salt and pepper shakers which he and my mother had been given as a wedding gift. *Boy is he in trouble if he makes my mother's favorite shaker set disappear!* I thought.

"Now, focus on just the salt and pepper shaker," he continued. "Don't worry about the hat. Concentrate hard. I am going to chant a phrase and you must repeat it right after me, exactly as I say it. And focus solely on the shakers. You are going to use your mind and the chant to help me get both of those shakers out from under the hat without ever touching it. Okay?"

We kids laughed at what was shaping up to be yet another of his corny jokes.

"Okay . . . yeah . . . got it; let's go!" we agreed.

65

Patricia, Britt, and Jimmy couldn't stop giggling as my father tried to begin the trick. "Quiet down, everyone," he said.

"Repeat after me, slowly . . . Oh wa."

"Oh wa," we all chanted.

"Ta na," he said.

"Ta na," we said.

"Si am."

"Si am," we chanted, keeping our eyes tightly closed. We were excited and prayed that when we opened our eyes, we would see the shakers actually rise up off of the table, like the scene from *The Exorcist*.

"Okay, now, say it a little faster!" he said. "Oh wa, ta na, si am." His voice got louder and more excited.

"Oh wa, ta na, si am," we gleefully repeated, getting more and more worked up. I squirmed in my chair, dying to open my eyes to sneak a peek at the levitating salt and pepper shakers. The anticipation was killing me. I was just about to take a small peek out of one eye, when my father barked, "Bernadette, pay attention!" His sudden outburst caused me to jump out of my seat and then close my eyes even tighter. I couldn't stop laughing.

"Say it even faster!" he demanded.

"Oh wa, ta na, si am, ohwa, tana, siam, ohwatanasiam.... oh wha tana siam, oh wha tana siam," we all chanted over and over and over again. Suddenly Chris, Mark, and Peggy began to laugh. *Why are they laughing?* I wondered.

The rest of the kids continued to chant. The laughing got harder, as the older kids enunciated the nonsensical words that made up the trick. The younger ones tried hard to make out what was so funny, but couldn't.

A few of us opened our eyes to see if the hat was actually rising, but it was still sitting firmly on the table. The other kids slowly enunciated the words,

"Oh what, an ass, I am, oh what, an ASS, I am!" The remaining kids started to laugh.

Finally able to decipher the actual phrase, Britt shrieked, "Dad, there is a curse word in that trick!" The whole table roared in laughter.

My father had been sitting at the end of the table laughing hysterically at the sight of his twelve children; eyes glued shut, faces scrunched from concentrating so hard, following his every command. He continued laughing as we realized what we were chanting and that the whole thing was a joke. My mother sat at the other end of the table shaking her head, flashing the sweetest of smiles, tickled pink at the idea that we had just been tricked.

My father cherished times spent with his kids and the simpler the activity, joke, or game, the more pleasure he got from it. Like the many years he convinced us that there was a watermelon, a special, huge watermelon, in one of the three fridges we had in our basement. He would tell us, "It is being ripened to the perfect sweetness and taste so it is just right when we're ready to feast on it." The entire table of kids would break out in hysteria, while he basked in the glory of yet another tall tale. For years, we believed the story—and then pretended to—until the younger kids were old enough to realize he'd been pulling their leg.

Whether it was fishing at the shore, camping along the Maryland coastline, or treating us to ice cream sundaes that were our reward after a recital or game, my father took great pride in the family he and my mother had created. He took even more pride in the idea that while he was making us laugh, he was also teaching us something about life.

I am not sure what the lesson was in, "Oh wa ta na si am." Maybe it was about not believing everything you are told. I thought it was about being able to laugh at yourself. Although he was reserved and serious, he always was able to laugh at himself. Any time we were hanging out, eating, or just enjoying each other's company, he would raise his hands to the heavens, look around at all of us, and say, "I wonder what the poor people are doing." A few of my brothers and sisters hated when he said that, especially in public. They never realized he was mocking himself, a poor man financially, but a wealthy man in terms of life, love, and family.

Throughout his long, eighty-four-year life, he strived to get each and every one of us to appreciate who we were, remember where we came from, and know how fortunate we were to have each other. He taught us how to take care of ourselves, take risks, challenge ourselves, and overcome adversity, no matter what. He wanted us to experience life head-on and never back down from it. I learned that lesson at the tender age of four, when he taught me how to swim.

My parents were longtime members of our local community swim and golf club, *Llanerch Country Club*. It was less than a mile from our house, which made it easy on both of them. We could walk together as a group and return home on our own, if needed. It also gave my mother and my father freedom from their dozen kids. They could leave us at the club under the watchful eyes of the lifeguards, pool attendants, and babysitters who worked there. Every day throughout the summer, from the time the pool opened at eight o'clock in the morning to the time they closed at nine o'clock at night, we spent the day swimming or playing basketball, badminton, or golf.

One hot summer day, six or seven of us were carrying on with other kids in the big pool. My parents found a shady spot under the large maple tree. My dad was reading the newspaper, and my mother was gabbing with her girlfriends. The lifeguards said I was too small for the big pool. They shooed me away from the bigger kids and made me go to the baby pool at the far end of the grounds. Walking away with my head hung low, I reluctantly made my way to the small body of water they called a pool. "We wouldn't want you to drown," they said, trying to justify the useless, cement-filled hole in the ground.

I hated the baby pool. It was for babies—crying babies, small babies, babies that wore diapers and even pooped in the pool. I was not a baby. I was a big girl! I couldn't help it if no one had taught me to swim yet. If they would teach me, I wouldn't have to hang out with the brats in the kiddies' pool. My brothers and sisters were either in the big pool or lying in a crib next to my mother under the tree. I was forced to play by myself. I wouldn't have it.

Determined and focused, my bottom falling out of my bathing suit, my long hair soaked and hanging over my eyes and face, I marched down the pavement, past the lifeguards to my mother at the other end of the pool. My father, absorbed in reading his *Philadelphia Inquirer*, never even noticed me walk up.

I yanked on my Mother's cover-up to get her attention and demanded, "Mommy, Mommy, I want to go in the big pool." I knew she would not be happy that I was disrupting her time with the girls, but I wanted to learn how to swim. And she or one of the kids was going to teach me. I wasn't going away until someone did.

"Sweetie," she said, "you're too small to go into the big pool. The big pool is for grownups. You like the baby pool, Bernadette."

"No, I don't!" I yelled.

"Don't raise your voice," she replied.

Persistently, I said, "I can swim. I can show you."

"Honey, you can't," she insisted. She stroked my face and pulled my wet hair away from my eyes. "Sweetie, I just had my hair done; I can't go into the pool today."

"But Theresa and Anne Marie are in the big pool," I pleaded. "They know how to swim. Tell them to teach me," pointing to my older sisters.

Whether it was to shut me up or to allow me to play with the big kids, my father jumped up from his chair with a determined look on his face, grabbed my hand, and without saying a word, walked me to the edge of the pool. I stood frozen, looking up at him, not sure what he was going to do.

"Kids, come here," he called to the others, who were carrying on in the shallow end of the big pool. They jumped out onto the pool deck. "Line up like so," he said. My father arranged each of us, from the tallest to the smallest, in a single line along the edge of the shallow end of the pool. I could only imagine what my mother was thinking.

Without uttering a word, he walked to the back of the line and, one by one, pushed each of us into the pool. I watched and grew nervous; I'd asked to learn how to swim, not drown. I didn't think he'd push me in. But when it was my turn, he placed his hand on my back and with a gentle push, tossed me forward into the water below.

Falling face first into the cold water, I panicked as I felt myself sinking. I kicked my legs and flapped my arms, not sure what it would do. I figured I had to do something. From deep below the water, I could hear my father yelling to me, "Sink or swim, Bernadette!" *Sink or swim*, I thought. *I don't want to sink*. Even so, I was sinking. I continued to kick and flap, wondering, *where did all of the kids go? Why isn't anyone coming to save me?* Finally, my face broke out of the water. I could breathe again.

I looked up and over to the edge and heard my father say, "Swim over to me, Bernadette." I could see the other kids standing around him and staring down at me as I flapped my way over to the edge. I reached up, grabbed the side firmly and pulled myself up. I looked at my father. He was beaming with pride. "Remember, young lady, there will be a lot of things in life that you think you can't do, and you will need to decide if you will sink or swim," he explained.

He pulled me up out of the pool, positioned me at the edge, and pushed me. This time, I wasn't scared. I kicked my legs and flapped my arms until I reached the surface and swam over to the edge once again.

Eventually, my father taught me to be a competitive swimmer. In fact, six of my siblings and I went on to compete and win over the next thirteen years.

That swim lesson taught me about character, mental toughness, confidence, and persistence. That day, my father taught me regardless of the challenges I faced, I had a choice; I could sink and drown or I could flap, splash, and face them head-on and swim.

My father was a complicated man of great contradiction. He was a man I feared and revered at the same time. He was my hero.

Born George L. Boas, my mother and his friends called him Fred. He got the name many years earlier while wearing his friend Fred's college letterman jacket. He was a tall, dark, and very handsome man. Standing more than six feet tall, he had a swagger, an aura, about him that commanded respect.

An only child, raised by two strict parents during the Great Depression, his impoverished childhood defined him as a man, husband, and father. As an only child, he was determined to have a large family—if God willed it.

My grandfather worked on the railroads and in the coal mines of Pennsylvania. He instilled an immutable work ethic in my father which he passed down to all of us. "You give everything you've got and you do it well," my father told us. "You can't have what you haven't earned." He would add, "If you want something, you have to work for it."

Working for what we wanted wasn't an option. We had to earn everything we received from him, including his respect.

I'll never forget the hot, humid summers during my junior high and high school years. If we were not swimming the day away at the pool, my father had us scrubbing, scraping, and cleaning every inch of his three-story office in downtown Philly.

Every morning for two weeks, he woke us at seven o'clock in the morning and packed our lunches along with a cooler of sodas, and drove us downtown to Camac Street. We'd see Philadelphia's City Hall building with its statue of William Penn perched on top, high and proud over the city, greeting all the passersby below.

When we pulled up in front of my father's office building, we looked up and greeted Willy with the liveliest; "Good morning!" we could muster. Then we were off. For the next six or seven hours, we'd work our way from the first floor to the third floor, scrubbing every office and bathroom with buckets of Pine Sol and water. We even put a fresh coat of paint on the walls and cleaned out the papers, files, or rolls of drafting paper that had piled up since the previous summer.

We hated those days. We wanted to be at the pool with our friends. We would swear, curse, and fight. It was hotter than Hell in that building. God forbid my father ever turns on the air conditioning; that was too costly. Although we nearly died from heat exhaustion, my father had the upper hand. All he had to do was tell us to be quiet, and we would shut up immediately. It worked every time, and it happened often over those two weeks.

We spent the rest of the summer scraping gum off the desks and chairs of my very own school. I finally asked my father, "Why do you guys have me cleaning your office every summer and then going into my own school to scrape gum off of my fellow students' desks? It's embarrassing and I don't get a break."

He would ask, "Do you want to go to Disney World for Christmas and go on camping trips?"

"Yes," I replied.

"Then you have to work for it," he said. "You and your brothers and sisters cleaning my office saves me from having to spend that money on hiring cleaners."

Being a typical, headstrong girl, I retorted, "What about cleaning the school?"

He firmly but calmly responded, "Do you want to go to school? Do you want to continue playing field hockey and softball?"

"Of course I do," I said with attitude.

"Then you have to pay for it. Your work at the school during the summer pays your tuition."

There was nothing more I could say.

It didn't matter if my parents had four kids or twelve kids; my father was determined to give us the best education, most competitive athletic programs, and whatever else we needed to become successful, happy adults. And since he would never, ever take a handout, he didn't want us to, either. Our weekly allowances were minuscule, but he took pride in the fact that he "rewarded" us for our hard work, not so much monetarily, but in principle.

On Friday nights, when he returned home from his office, my father would go into the living room, get comfortable in his oversized chair in the corner of the room, and catch up on the daily news splashed across the pages of the *Philadelphia Inquirer*. When he finished, he would yell, "Allowance!" We'd run into the living room and sit in front of him on the floor. Like a proud, wealthy man preparing to spread his fortune, he would call us to him one at a time. He would say, "Hold your hands out wide, really wide. You don't want to drop any of it." We'd chuckle like we had the week before and place cupped hands together so he could drop the pile of nickels into our palms.

Every week until we graduated from high school, my father gave us nickels, one for each year of our age. When we were seventeen and seniors in high school, our big, whopping allowance added up to eighty-five cents!

My father knew our nickels wouldn't buy much. Yet, each time he dropped the coins into our hands, he would chuckle and say, "Don't spend it all in one store, now."

I would roll my eyes and walk away.

Our allowance was never meant to make us rich. It was to teach us we had to work hard—in the classroom, on the playing field, in the workplace— to earn someone else's riches. That lesson taught me to question the value I bring to everything I do, because I believed that if I did not deliver value, I did not deserve anything in return.

My father never knew how deeply his lessons influenced his children, especially me, until one evening during my senior year of high school.

That year is a blur to me now. But I do remember I worked hard in my classes. I never missed a day of school, because I had a major crush on Tommy, a senior basketball player. I remember that I excelled in field hockey and swimming. My usual babysitting, gift wrapping, and telemarketing jobs were minimal that year and I couldn't afford the bell bottoms and Hush Puppies I wanted. When it came time to buy tickets to the annual sports awards banquet, I didn't have the money.

It was the last day to buy tickets. My homeroom teacher, Mr. Maguire, approached me in the hallway and with a solemn look asked, "Bernadette, why haven't you bought a ticket to your awards dinner? You and your varsity field hockey team will be recognized."

"I don't have the money," I said, honestly.

He looked at me with pity, which made my skin crawl. I fought back the tears that welled up inside me. He said, "Why don't you ask your parents for it? They would want you to go."

As much as I knew what Mr. Maguire was saying was true, I also knew my father's high standards. We had to earn the money, because we didn't accept handouts. During my senior year, I spent very little time working and more time playing. Asking my father for a handout was not going to happen. Plus, I was intimidated by my father, not because of his strong presence, but because of his stern, firm beliefs. I was sassy but I never challenged him. None of us did.

That evening at home, Jimmy, Michael, Patricia, and I were sitting in the den watching television when we heard my parents talking. Their voices carried loudly from the kitchen through the dining room and into the den. My brother Michael remarked, "Oh boy, someone must be in trouble."

My father yelled out, "Bernadette, come here please!"

I got up from the floor, anxious about whatever I did to have my parents all worked up. The other kids started with the usual, "Uh-oh, you're in trouble!"

I kicked my brother as I walked past him and headed to the kitchen.

My mother sat at the table, her head hung low, and I heard a whimper of a cry coming from her. I asked, "What's wrong Mom?"

She barely lifted her head when my father asked in what was a soft, shaken voice, "Bernadette, why didn't you come to your mother or me about buying a ticket to your awards banquet?"

Unable to speak, I stood frozen against the refrigerator. "Bernadette, your mother and I just realized you have never come to us and asked us for anything. Not ever," he continued, his voice cracking.

With tears flowing down my face, all I could muster was, "I know, Dad, but I didn't work for it, so I didn't earn it."

His face turned white. He leaned back in his chair, ran his fingers through his thinning hair, and let out the biggest sigh I had ever heard from him. He called me to him, pulled my face down into his chest for a hug, and handed me the thirty-five dollars. "Tell Mr. Maguire thank you for us," he said. "Now go and watch TV with the kids." I quietly exited the room, and nothing more was ever said about it.

Years later, when I recalled that time with him, he said, "I never realized until that moment how much you kids listened to my lessons and how seriously you followed them."

Whether we were cleaning his office or the classrooms, babysitting, running paper routes, or helping quadriplegic kids at the local children's home, we never forgot my father's life lessons. They included everything from being on time, leaving places better than you found them, teamwork, debating and negotiation, dealing with confrontation head-on, and much more. He made sure we knew how to dress for success, socially and professionally. He would say, "You can get in anywhere, if you are dressed up. You won't be allowed in if you are dressed down." Those little tidbits helped me achieve both my social and professional success over the years. He never imagined I would choose to follow other people's examples and behaviors, take on a foreign persona, thinking it would give me the success I wanted so badly.

I was never daddy's little girl, but more like a son. He only voiced his disappointment in me and my attitude once over the years. That one comment, however, would be the beginning of the end of who I was at the time. It was too bad he had not said it to me years earlier. Instead, his "seventh son" took her hero's teachings and manipulated them to her own liking.

Chapter 8

THE SEVENTH SON

Most daughters are daddy's girls—adored, coddled, and protected. My father had a lot of 'daddy's girls,' six to be exact: Mary, the oldest girl, was his 'duchess'; Peggy, his 'Streisand'; Theresa was his 'Saint', or 'Sister Theresa', as we called her; Anne Marie was his 'Peanut'; Patricia, the youngest, well, when he didn't stop to think, he would mistakenly call her by any one of our names at any given time.

I was 'Babe,' my father's dreamy-eyed, risk-taking girl who dreamed of the big office, big job, big travel, big house, and big money. Dad was okay with that, and ever since I was ten, he knew I was different from his other daughters. He knew that unlike them, I would get my big husband and big family later in life. He knew my dreams were too big for just anyone. It would take time and patience to find just the right man. First, I'd have to conquer the world; then I could conquer a family. My father equipped me with all the tools I needed to do just that, including a different kind of father-daughter partnership.

I never felt like a daddy's girl. Intimidated by his strict and reserved manner, I spent most of my childhood tiptoeing around him as opposed to cuddling up to him. I often avoided him rather than engage in play or sport with him. I can remember getting into trouble at school, as I often did, fearing the confrontation I would have with him when he got home from work. After dinner, my mother would share anything that occurred that day, including any mischief we kids got into. As soon as he excused us from the table, I would go right to my room, praying I'd avoid his discipline.

Already lying in bed, I would hear him and my mother talking in the living room below. Sometimes, he would yell out for me to come downstairs. Other times, he would come to me. One night, he decided to come and see me in my bedroom. I could hear him march across the living room floor and up the wooden staircase.

I jumped out of bed to turn off the light, then jumped back into bed, pulled the covers up to my neck, and closed my eyes tight—but not so tight that he could tell I was faking. As he turned the door handle, I took a deep breath and lay there, still as I could. His presence flooded the room as he stood in the doorway. I could feel him looking over at me. I knew he wouldn't turn on the light in case I was indeed asleep. He waited a few seconds more and then left, shutting the door behind him. I exhaled, relieved that he didn't wake me up to scold me for the incident with my teacher, Mr. Bushy. Then I grew anxious about avoiding him, as he was a man who never forgot.

The next morning at breakfast, I had to face him. As always, I was surprised by his response.

"What happened at school yesterday that caused you to be sent to detention?" he demanded.

Oh boy, I thought, *if he ever knew all the times I've been sent to detention.* "I left his class so I could see Peggy's play!" I said.

"Why didn't you ask for your teacher's permission?"

"I did and he said I couldn't go and watch her. Then he said he didn't care if she was my sister. I had to stay in class. I didn't agree, as this could be one of few times I could see her, so I left."

I expected him to be angry at me for disrespecting authority. But he simply said, "I can't say I liked what Mr. Bushy said to you but he is your teacher, and you need to listen to him."

The next day at school, I learned that my father had called Mr. Bushy to tell him that he did not like how he treated me. Dad said he did not advocate what I did, but he wasn't going to allow him to punish me, either. I was floored, but I shouldn't have been surprised.

My father had a temper and could be very unreasonable, especially in the eyes of a teenager. He would bark orders from his living room chair or his recliner in the den. Sometimes, it came from his bed if my mother didn't get a chance to talk to him the night before. Other times, it came from the breakfast table. Occasionally, he yelled before he thought, but when he did, he would listen to us until he had the whole story. Though at times he used the belt and the slap, he was fair in doling out punishment. He didn't do it just to do it. I realized that years later, and found myself questioning why I was ever afraid of him.

My father's personality was larger than life. Years later, I learned he was also a kind, gentle, and vulnerable man who adored and worshipped his wife and children. One of my favorite memories is of him and my mother sitting on the couch in my first apartment. As they sat there, watching TV and talking, they held each other's hand. I would never have believed it had I not seen it for myself. That moment changed everything I thought I knew about my father. I obviously did not know all there was to know about him.

Over the years, I had misinterpreted his lessons about hard work and earning what you get. I had created and internalized a feeling of unworthiness. My father never forbade me to ask for money or told me I couldn't go to a camp or awards banquet. I told *myself* these things, not fully grasping the lessons he was trying to teach me. He merely wanted all of us to work hard so we would appreciate the things we received. He never did or said anything to instill my feelings of unworthiness. I created these beliefs within myself.

It was me who allowed my own negative mindset and belief systems, or what I call my inner 'bitch,' to conjure up these insecurities and fuel these feelings as a child and later, as an adult.

It wouldn't be until I was in my twenties, living away from home, that he and I would establish a relationship I never dreamed of as a child. I wasn't just 'daddy's little girl'; I became more like his seventh son.

It began when he and my mother drove from Philadelphia to South Florida for my college graduation. I was planning to celebrate with my friends and their families. I never thought my parents would make the long drive to attend my graduation. It would be too costly a trip and it would keep them away from home and the younger kids too long.

One evening, as I sat in the lounge area of my dormitory, one of the girls in the room next to mine yelled, "Bernadette, your mother is on the phone!" *My mother*, I thought to myself. *Oh my god, what is wrong? What happened to my father?*

I threw my homework to the floor, dropped the soda bottle in my hand and raced down the hall to my room.

My father had the first of several heart attacks when I was in my senior year of high school. Since then, anytime a family member called, I panicked. From that fear, I began to force my family members to say, "I love you," before hanging up the phone. "You don't know," I told them, "That phone call could be your last chance to tell someone you love them." It took a long time for my brothers and sisters to get used to it; a few of them still can't bring themselves to say it. By my senior year of college, saying "I love you" was a natural part of my phone conversations with my mother and father. Just as natural as my father's usual question, "So, how's your love life?"

When I reached my dorm room, I grabbed the phone from my roommate's hand. "What's wrong with Dad?" I blurted out.

"Dad's fine and so is everyone else," my mother replied. "Your father and I were just talking and wanted to finalize our plans to come down for your graduation."

"You're coming down? Here? For how long?" I asked, incredulous.

"Why are you so surprised? You're graduating college, Bernadette."

"I don't know. I just never considered you guys would come all of the way down here to see me," I said.

Disregarding that remark, Mom continued, "We'll probably stay five or six days. Your father wants to go fishing and you and I can hang out at the pool."

We talked for another five minutes or so, and all I could think about was the discussion she would have with my father. *She didn't think we would come down to see her,* I imagined her saying to him. I began to panic.

Hang out, with me? I thought. *Are they kidding? I have no idea what I would say or do with them. Mom? Yes. Dad? No way!*

I felt sad for thinking that way. Here were two people whom I adored in so many ways and had always wanted to have all to myself. Yet, here I was, freaking out because they were coming to spend time with me. This thought made me happy. I felt special. My parents were taking time from their busy schedules and the younger kids, who were still in high school, to drive 1,800 miles to see me. My happiness turned to excitement and then to planning. I needed to figure out what in the world to do with them.

My parents' first visit to Florida to see me was a turning point in my relationship with my father. Staring out the big bay windows of my dormitory lounge, I saw their white Volare pull onto the campus and down the main drive to my dorm. I had been sitting there for hours, watching for them. When I finally saw their old car pull down the main road of the campus entrance, I flew off the couch, threw open the heavy metal dormitory door, and raced down the three flights of stairs to the visitors' parking lot.

I'm not sure why that moment was so significant for me. Maybe it was because for the first time in my entire life, I was the center of my parents' attention. I felt completely loved and special. Even if we did nothing during their stay, it was just going to be them and me.

I ran through the parking lot to my father's car. I didn't even wait for him to open his door. I threw the driver's side door open and gave him the biggest bear hug he had ever had—right there while he was still turning off the engine. My mother had already gotten out of the car when I ran around to her.

Here they were, in my new hometown, on my turf, in my dorm, with my friends. For the next several days and nights we spent time talking and laughing, debating and challenging one another. My father took time to sit with me and look through my college photos, never judging my friends or the antics we engaged in.

Each morning, he got up bright and early and went off, alone, to Alligator Alley, twenty miles south. There, he'd sit alongside the road, reel casted, to enjoy the peace and quiet of the marshes. When he didn't go fishing, he checked out local coffee shops. On one of his long, peaceful drives south to Fort Lauderdale; he'd stumbled upon a topless donut shop along Federal Highway. My father certainly loved women.

He'd return around four o'clock each afternoon, just in time for dinner. During that long, restful week, I had the opportunity to sit for hours with my parents and get to know my father, the man I knew very little about while growing up.

During my graduation dinner, I watched my father beaming as he shared our family stories with my friends and their parents. As I listened to him talk about the girl I had been and how proud he was of the woman I had become, I was overcome with emotion. I realized how absurd it was to spend so many nights pretending to be asleep, to avoid having a conversation with him, afraid that I would disappoint him. Why had I allowed my mind to play games with my self-confidence? Why had I built up those negative beliefs about who I was, what I gave back to people, and what I contributed to the world?

That trip to Florida was the turning point for my father and me. We were no longer just father and daughter; we were now friends.

A few months after my graduation, and now in my own apartment, I got a call from my father. "Babe, I wanted to come down next weekend to do some fishing," he began. "Are you gonna be around?"

"Absolutely! Come on down!" I said, excitedly. That first solo trip was the first of many weekend trips he would make to spend time fishing along the Alley or Key Largo or search from Palm Beach to Key West for the best key lime pie.

Our time together became routine and so did our itinerary. I'd pick him up from the airport, drive along Federal Highway, stop at various restaurants for turtle soup with sherry, and a drink at the top of the Hyatt Hotel on the Seventeenth Street Bridge. There, in the rotating lounge, we'd watch the boats and people go by as the floor rotated a full 360 degrees every hour.

Over the years we spent many hours discussing our lives. We challenged each other's beliefs, from his view of women in the house and workplace, to politics, to the state of young people today. I told him about my troubled love life and my career successes. I openly shared details about my social life and athletic feats, as well as my fear of aging and new challenges. We spent hours discussing our travels, whether it was my trips to New York, San Diego, Vietnam, or Dubai, or our common visits to Ireland, Mexico, and England. My father expressed his desire to visit his favorite place on earth one last time before he died. And so, in 2000, when he was eighty years old, he and I set off on an eight-day trip to Paris, France.

My brothers and sisters thought I was crazy. "How are you going to deal with him for eight, long days?" they wondered. They didn't understand that he and I had grown to thoroughly enjoy each other's company. I saw it as an honor that he asked me to accompany him. I knew his memory was jumbled and his physical capacities were becoming limited, but this was a once-in-a-lifetime opportunity. Eventually, my siblings voiced regret that it wasn't them sharing that experience with him.

And what an experience it was! Each morning, we visited the local café for croissants and jelly. Then it was off to catch the "Metro," the subway on which we would make our way through the city. One day, my father sat for more than six hours on a hard plastic chair, reading the local paper, insisting I take my time roaming the marble halls of the Lourve Museum. We would find a brasserie, or "brewery," along the Seine, where we would lunch on salmon, cheese, and wine. We would return to the hotel before dark, exhausted by the endless walking and excitement. We spent hours each morning and night recapping our adventures. I was amazed at his energy and desire to show me *his* Paris. Each night, we sat on our individual twin beds, in one of the smallest hotel rooms I had ever seen, writing about our adventures in our personal journals and reviewing our maps to plan out the next day's activities.

The long days of walking the tree-lined streets of Paris took their toll on my elderly father. I cried when he collapsed in his church pew, weak from miles of walking, at Notre Dame on Easter Sunday. I was wrecked by fear when I found him lying on the streets of Montmartre, after falling off his small café seat. Most nights, I cried myself to sleep as I listened to his erratic breathing and gurgling, his sleeping body weary after a grueling day of sightseeing.

Still, each day he mustered the strength to walk the streets of Paris, overjoyed to show me the city he loved. I rediscovered a patience and calm I had not felt in years. He was determined to make this trip his most memorable. We were close before that trip to Paris, but even closer after we returned. Our relationship grew to a point where he would simply pick up the phone and say, "I'm coming down to fish!" And I would wait excitedly for my best friend to arrive.

He told me about his corporate days at Scott Paper when he led a group of drafting executives. He talked about the challenges of starting, running, and maintaining his own drafting business.

He taught me about professionalism, business acumen, leadership, dealing with the boys' club, and how to leverage hard work and great results for great gains, whether it was for money, power, or position. If he was ever disappointed in me for the woman I became in pursuit of those gains, he mentioned it only once, shortly before he died. "Babe," he said. "I'm just afraid your ambitions will prevent you from finding true happiness, true love. I pray to God you do not let that happen."

My father, my *hero,* would be very proud of the woman I have become. I had to go through some ugly, painful, hurtful times before I would become that woman. By the time my father died in 2005, his 'seventh son' had become one of 'daddy's little girls,' even though others could only see a royal bitch.

Chapter 9

FREEDOM IN A TRASH BAG

In the middle of a dead sleep, I felt someone grab my arm and pull me up off the couch. Hung over and exhausted, I forced my eyes open and looked up to see Michael standing over me. I could tell by the look on his face he was pissed. "Hey, what's up?" I asked, nonchalantly.

I had gone to bed at four o'clock that morning. It was obvious from the smeared mascara on my cheeks and my smoke-filled clothes that I had spent the previous night partying, not preparing for my upcoming move.

"What's up?" he snapped back. Michael had expected me back in Philly two days earlier to pack for our long drive to Florida. We were due to start classes at Florida Atlantic University (FAU) in Boca Raton in just a few days. He hadn't planned on driving two hours to my summer beach house in Wildwood, New Jersey, to drag my butt out of bed and into a cold shower. "Let's go!" he yelled, as he pulled me up and dragged me into the bathroom. He put me in the bathtub and turned on the shower.

"Damn it, Michael!" I screamed, as ice cold water rushed from the faucet.

"Look, you've partied enough this summer. It's time to face reality!" he barked. *Face reality?* I thought. The man had lived on Florida beaches the whole year before. On paper, he was enrolled in oceanography school, but in reality, he spent his time partying up and down the coast from West Palm to South Miami.

Refreshed from the cold shower, I started to pack. I told Michael about all the farewell parties being thrown for me; the Hand Avenue house gang, the Sharkey's Lifeguard Bar crowd, and the Diamond Beach friends I had met that summer had plans to wish me "bon voyage" with lots of booze! I could tell from the look on Michael's face that he wanted to party, too. He never missed a good party. "We're staying, at least until tomorrow," he said abruptly. Then he ran to his car to get his swim trunks and sunglasses.

Minutes later, we were headed to *Diamond Beach* for an afternoon of fun at the *Barefoot Bar*.

Michael, or "Mikey" as others called him, and I became fast friends a year earlier when Theresa and Anne Marie introduced us at the Dade House, a club in Philadelphia. I was too young to drink, but the club paid no mind. The bouncers at the door brushed over our fake licenses and shuffled us past the cops at the door.

Michael, with his long, black, curly hair, colorful baggy pants, tight polyester shirts, and white linen disco shoes, looked like a white version of Rick James. He was always the life of the party, and he threw some of the best parties around. I knew the minute we met that we would be fast friends. I would never be lonely and bored with him. Those were two things Michael knew nothing about.

The next morning, still hung over, we made the ninety-minute drive to my parents' house in Philly. My parents would be waiting, since they had expected to send us off the day before.

I had waited so long for this moment. In less than twenty-four hours, I would be on my own and free to be whoever I wanted to be. I would be just Bernadette, no longer one of 'the Boas kids,' one of a dozen, or the milkman's daughter. Just Bernadette. I imagined myself as *Fanny Brice* in *Funny Girl*, announcing, *"I'm going to live and live NOW! Get what I want, I know how! One roll for the whole shebang! One throw that bell will go clang, eye on the target and wham, one shot, one gunshot and bam! Hey world, here I am!"* I was so excited that for a moment, I forgot how bad I felt.

When we reached my parents' house, I jumped out of the car, raced into the house, slammed the door behind me, and ran upstairs to the bedroom I shared with my youngest sister, Patricia. I went inside and started emptying drawers into the middle of the room. I sorted the things I would take with me from those things I would throw away. *What do they wear in South Florida?* I thought. *I won't need my long coats, will I? Does it get cold down there? Will I need my ski outfits? I'm sure Floridians ski*, I chuckled to myself.

I was so excited, I couldn't think straight. Patricia heard me banging drawers and came up to help. I told her I needed to do it myself but invited her to keep me company. Excitedly, she jumped onto her bed and laughed as I frantically walked in and out of the closet, emptying drawers, packing up my art supplies, and packing all my worldly possessions into large, green trash bags.

"Why are you packing your things in trash bags?" She asked.

"Do you have suitcases that I am unaware of?" I snapped, unintentionally. Growing up, our family had traveled frequently up and down the east coast. But because we camped most of the time, we only required duffle bags, not suitcases. Of all the things that were passed down from sibling to sibling, suitcases were never on the list. Trash bags it was.

"Why are you rushing so much?" she asked. "Are you in that much of a rush to get rid of us?" Her words stopped me in my tracks.

"No! It's just a long drive and we have to be there by Friday," I said, dismissing the fact that I would desperately miss her and Britt. It was easier to cut ties and run than to stick around for a long, sad, and tearful good-bye.

I tossed each full trash bag to Michael, who was waiting at the bottom of the stairs. He grabbed several at a time and piled them into the back seats of his 1972, two-door, green Pontiac. By the time he finished, Michael could barely see out the back window. Finally, I had just one more drawer to pack. It contained all my books, reports, and memorabilia from school, including my high school senior year book.

Feeling nostalgic, I sat down on my childhood bed and flipped through the pages to look through the photos of old friends. "Check me out in my field hockey team picture!" I said to Patricia. She came and sat next to me on my bed. "You won't believe the comments these guys wrote about me." *You really are a special person and never change...Joanne, Stay as nice and sweet as you are...Kim. It's great knowing a person like you...Diane. You are a sweet girl, don't ever change...Frank.* We both got a big kick from reading them aloud.

High school already seemed like a lifetime ago. Even on graduation day, I had sensed that I was changing and was no longer the girl that my classmates had known. Most of my friends were staying close to home, but I had always dreamed about moving away. By the time we graduated, I craved independence from our small town, our small crowd, and the small dreams others had.

I looked around the room to make sure I wasn't forgetting anything. I caught a glimpse of Patty Cake, a stuffed monkey I had won for Patricia when she was just eight years old. Without hesitating, I grabbed the monkey, wiped tears from my eyes, tossed the yearbook into the last trash bag, and headed downstairs.

I raced out the back door and down the porch steps toward the car. I jumped into the front seat and slammed the door behind me and squealed, "Yeeeee-haaah!" Then, in a flash, I realized I had forgotten the single, or maybe double, most important thing in my life. I threw the car door back open and leapt from the front seat as if it were on fire. I flew back into the house to the den where my father and mother were sitting with Patricia and Britt.

"You weren't going to leave without saying goodbye, were you?" Patricia asked, her voice shaking with emotion.

"Absolutely not!" The excitement just got to me," I explained. I pulled her to me and gave her a huge, tight hug and whispered, "I love ya." Tears ran down my face. Patricia was my heart and soul. Words can't really describe how I feel about her.

Before I broke down completely, I went over to Britt and gave him a quick hug and peck on the cheek. He was a young man now so he didn't need his big sister getting all mushy over him.

The two of them, now fourteen and twelve, were like my children. I had raised them, looked out for them, and adored them. And they adored me. As a farewell gift, they gave me an oversized card that read, "To our 5-F sister!" When I asked them how it went from '3-F' to '5-F,' they chuckled and said, "Well, you are not only foxy, flakey and far-out but now you are far-away in Florida!" I couldn't help but laugh and then cry.

Saying goodbye to my parents was both heartbreaking and exciting. They were happy and sad for me, as well. Just a year before graduating high school, though I had researched out-of-state universities, determined to fly away to find my freedom, I made one of the hardest decisions of my seventeen years.

I decided to stay at home with my parents. "There are plenty of good schools right here Dad," I explained.

"Not the schools that will allow you to have your own place, make new friends, and let you see different parts of the world!" he argued. He didn't understand why his sassy, spunky, and precocious daughter was giving up on her dreams of conquering the world.

Quite simply, I was afraid, though I didn't tell him that.

In the early part of my senior year, my father had the first of several severe heart attacks. It scared me to death. Not just me, but my mother and siblings, as well. *How could I leave them now? What if something happened and I was hundreds of miles away? Who would take care of mom and the little ones?* I replayed those thoughts over and over again in my mind.

I allowed that fear to keep me frozen in place there in Philadelphia. I found myself crippled by the unknown: *would he have another heart attack? Would the next one kill him, and what if I am far away?* During that long year, while I attended a local university, my father often asked me, "What are you going to do, stay here at home and wait until I die? Bernadette, you need to go and live your own life. You can't live mine!"

"I will Dad, I promise," I replied. Following my heart and his words, I was packing my life in trash bags and preparing to head south to create that life.

Standing tall in front of me, arms outstretched, he couldn't have been prouder. My father, who was well-read and well-traveled, was adamant that all of us get a college education. But he was even more adamant that we learn what life was all about first-hand from our own mistakes and successes. The thing he wanted most for us was to travel the world. He believed that experiencing countries, cities, architecture, cuisine, and different cultures was the best education. He often said, "The world is your classroom; don't forget that." I never would.

Now, on a sunny Wednesday morning in 1981, I was packed and ready to go out and see the world. Stretching my arms as far as they would go, I hugged each of my parents tightly, kissed them on the cheek, and whispered, "I love you so much, no words can express." Fighting back the tears, I pulled away from them quickly and ran out to the waiting car and Michael.

As we pulled out of our long driveway, I glanced back to see my parents standing on our big front porch, waving good-bye. Patricia and Britt ran off the steps and onto the front pavement, screaming, "Bye!" and waving their arms so hard I thought their shoulders would fall out of their sockets. Once down Eagle Road and out of sight, I let the tears flow. I could hear my dad's voice prompting, "Shoulders back, chest out. Now, just go!"

Fifteen years later, after I had visited several continents, achieved impressive career titles, and made a nice chunk of money, my father asked me, nonchalantly, "Aren't you glad you didn't wait until I was dead?" We both broke out in laughter. I was glad; that move to Florida changed everything for me. What I didn't expect was that it would change me for the worse.

Twenty hours later, sitting cramped, in the bucket seats of Michael's two-door sports car, I was ready to get there, already. We had brought only a few cassettes to keep us entertained. Michael insisted on three or four cassettes of Rick James' music. The only cassette I owned was Barbra Streisand. We replayed them over and over and over. By the time we reached Boca Raton, we were sick of hearing them.

Michael made a sharp turn and veered off the highway and up a ramp toward a major thoroughfare. *Not another potty break,* I thought. The car raced by a highway exit sign that read, Glades Road/Boca Raton. Boca Raton! *Oh my God! We're here! I am just blocks from my new life, my new future, my new me!* I could hardly stand the excitement.

A road sign directed us to FAU's main entrance. "Yeahhh!!" I screamed.

"You would think you never went away on a trip before!" Michael said.

"This isn't just a trip, Michael; this is the beginning of a whole new life!" I shouted, rocking back and forth, anxious to get there.

I glanced out the window. Beyond the entrance sign was a large three-story building. I imagined it was an administration building stretching out its arms and welcoming us to our new life. Michael made a left turn and drove down the palm tree-lined road that led us directly in front of that three-story building. He pulled the car up to the turnabout and said, "You're here!"

"Where?" I asked.

"Your new home. This is your dorm," he chuckled.

"Really? Yeee-haa, let's go!" I shouted, jumping out of the car door like a kid going to Disney World for the first time.

FAU had everything I was looking for in a college: a small student body (about 4,500 at the time), an 'everyone knows everyone' atmosphere, and a campus that was small enough that I could get around without a car. I was eighteen and still didn't have my driver's license.

Cars and driver's licenses were two things my parents refused to give us, even as a high school graduation present. They had made it very clear that we weren't allowed to get our license or have a car until we graduated high school. If we wanted a car, we would have to pay for it ourselves. I was not going to pay for a car if I could help it. I was more interested in spending my money on summer beach houses, ski trips, and weekend get-a-ways. Turns out, I would soon discover, I needed the money I had saved to keep up with the Joneses (the very rich kids of FAU). *I'll find friends that drive,* I reasoned.

It was just days before I began to feel like Dorothy in *The Wizard of Oz,* out of place, lost, alone and definitely not in Kansas anymore. FAU and Boca Raton were worlds apart from the middle-class, suburban community where I was raised. It was like the east coast version of Beverly Hills and Rodeo Drive. The wealthy and wanna-be rich strutted around campus and town in their stiletto heels and Louis Vuitton bags. My college friends drove Mercedes, flew to class in helicopters, or had their chauffeurs drop them off. I felt like Julia Roberts in the movie, *Pretty Woman.* I shopped in stores I couldn't afford and spent money I didn't have, in order to keep up with the other kids. That's when everything began to change. I realized that for me to be somebody in that town and on that campus, I had to become someone I wasn't.

I learned to wear the mask and persona of a rich kid. It didn't take long for me to start craving the money and power the rich kids had. I wanted it, no matter who I had to become.

My family prepared me well to take on the world and conquer the goals I had for my life. Boca and FAU fueled my passions, dreams, and ever-growing ambitions. What my family had never considered was that a small town, nestled in the beautiful palm trees and white sandy beaches of South Florida, would transform their '5-F' sister/daughter into a ruthless bitch. I never once considered that I was discarding the loving, caring values my parents had instilled in me. My greed had a mind of its own.

Chapter 10

A BITCH IS BORN

"Can I help you?" I asked the woman wearing the fur wrap as she approached the cash register. She turned up her nose and glared at me. From the look on her face, you would have thought I'd just told her that her husband was cheating on her.

"Of course you can, young lady! I have been waiting on someone to take care of me and get my packages to the car!" she snapped.

Stunned by her brazen attitude, I forced a smile and replied graciously, "I would be more than happy to help you Ma'am." *Damn, how dare she talk to me like that?* I thought. I had stepped away from the register for less than a minute and this woman, dripping in diamonds, was lashing out at me for no reason.

She threw the items from her basket onto the counter and handed me her credit card. "Bring them out to the car when you're done," she ordered, pointing to the exit. Before I could respond, she turned and walked away.

Who the hell does she think I am? One of her servants? How dare she throw her merchandise at me and command that I bring her packages out to her? I am not her lackey! After all, I thought, *this is a Five and Dime store, not Neiman Marcus or Barney's. But it is Boca,* I reminded myself. *Most of the people here are that way.* Still fuming, I rang up her order like a good little girl.

What pissed me off even more was that this woman was not much older than me, maybe twenty-four or twenty-five. She didn't even know what season it was. It was fifty-eight degrees outside, too warm to wear a fur wrap. *What a bitch!* I thought to myself. And damn proud to be one, too!

I did exactly as she commanded and brought her packages out to her nice, shiny Mercedes. I briefly considered "forgetting" to give her back her credit card out of revenge. But my conscience wouldn't let me. I delivered her packages, her card, and receipt. *She may be a bitch*, I said to myself, *but it doesn't mean I have to be.*

I couldn't believe how bitchy the women—and men—were in this town. Everyone was rude, selfish, and of course, rich. It didn't matter that they were bitches; they got what they wanted. I was learning that money talks, and it became a language I wanted to speak too.

The woman in Shoprite that day was just one of many 'Boca Bitches,' as they were commonly called. I seemed to run into these women—and men—every day. They were well-kept, ferociously mean-spirited, arrogant, and bitchy! Their attitudes, though offensive, intrigued me. *How is it that they can be so incredibly nasty and still get everything they want?* I wondered. I continued to watch and learn and eventually, imitate the Boca Bitch. I thought, *if it worked for them, it just might work for me.*

I was sitting on the patio at the Boca Hotel with a group of college friends—Debra, Sam, Tom, Kathy, Sarah, and Laura. We had just graduated from college and were treating ourselves to a celebratory brunch of mimosas, Bloody Mary's, assorted pastries, salmon, lobster, caviar, and seasonal fruits. While we ate, we watched the yachts and boats sail along the Intracoastal Inlet.

A group of twenty-something spoilers came in from a day of sunbathing, sailing, and shopping. Freshly tanned and arms full of packages, they sat down at the table next to us. They paid no mind to anyone around them, including us, completely lost in their own chatter. Suddenly, one of the young women in the group snapped her fingers. I turned to see who she was snapping at.

She was snapping her fingers at the waitress, who was tending to another table. Holding a cell phone to her ear and chomping on a wad of gum, she yelled to the waitress. The server graciously turned toward her and signaled that she would be right with her. Incredulous, the young woman, still holding the phone, got up from her table, walked up to the waitress, and said loudly, "I have been waiting and I need a drink, now!" The waitress apologized to the people she was serving and followed the girl to her table. Her friends smiled smugly, as if she had every right to treat the waitress like a piece of dirt.

I wanted to jump up, grab the girl by the throat, and choke her. What I really would have liked was for the waitress to escort her back to the table, tell her to sit down, and wait her turn. Unfortunately, she buckled under the pressure and gave the bitch what she wanted.

Disgusted, yet curiously intrigued by the deference given to these Boca Bitches, I asked the waitress, "How do you put up with them?"

"It's okay," she said. "They tip a lot." That, they did. Not to reward the service of the wait staff, more to show up their friends. I found myself studying these people and even acting like them myself. I studied their every move and interactions with people, from restaurant servers and store clerks, to fellow patrons and even their "friends".

I began to notice that even my friends threw their weight around, copped arrogant attitudes, ridiculed and judged each other. They wanted the attention and responsiveness too. Most were convinced that being a bitch was the way to get it.

Everyone who was anyone in Boca could be found at the polo grounds every Saturday from January through April. Hours before the first strike of the mallet, lines of cars tailgated and people picnicked on the pristine grounds. Some days, a live band played on the patio of the clubhouse. Most days, music poured from the convertible Mercedes, BMWs, Porches, and Bentleys that lined the field.

The women wore Lilly Pulitzer sundresses, Chanel flats, and Gucci sunglasses, while the men wore Polo shirts, J. Crew pants and Dockers shoes.

They sipped champagne from cut crystal glasses, snacked on fresh chocolate-dipped strawberries, and dined on assorted meats and cheeses. For me, it was yet another scene from *Pretty Woman*.

My friends and I preferred trendy dresses, cropped pants, sandals, and khakis and starched shirts for the guys. But our attitudes were the same. We packed our picnic basket with mimosas, peel-and-eat-shrimp, cheese, crackers, and sweets. We were all set for a day of men on horses, the cracking of the mallet, and the ritual stomping of divots at halftime.

The real entertainment, though, was people watching. My friends and I took to the stands to watch the match from up high. I was dating one of the polo players, in from Texas, so I wanted to pay more attention to the actual match on this day.

Seated directly behind us was a group dressed in beat-up jeans and t-shirts. Rolling her eyes at them, my friend Donna announced loud enough for them to hear, "They must be from Pompano Beach or West Boca."

Laughing at her comment, I asked, with a voice full of disdain, "Who brings hotdogs and potato chips to the polo grounds?" Not concerned if they heard us or not, we laughed mockingly and turned our backs to them.

By the time the polo match got underway, our 'bitch' walls were up. We continued to glare at and snub the group behind us at every opportunity. It was obvious they were offended by our haughtiness, but we didn't care. We enjoyed turning our noses up at people we thought weren't as good as us. We took great pleasure in acting superior to everyone around us. They weren't impressed, just pissed.

At halftime, we headed to the field to stomp divots, the highlight of the day. Every man and woman, and the well-dressed kids who accompanied them, would race onto the field. Unhindered by their thousand-dollar outfits and shoes, they would raise their dresses or pant legs and stomp the mounds of grass and dirt the swinging mallets had dug up during the match. It was a sight to see—and I loved watching it each and every time.

As the third chukker got underway, I sat back on the bleachers with my friends. Suddenly, I felt liquid running down the back of my dress and into my panties, completely soaking me. I jumped up and shrieked, "What the hell?" Twisting around to look at the back of my dress, I saw a pinkish red stain from the middle of my back to the skirt of the pale blue and white dress.

I shook my dress and looked up to see the Pompano Beach group staring at me, panic streaked across their faces. One of the younger teenage girls sat there with a near-empty, blue plastic cup in her hand. Without a word, I grabbed it from her and saw a few drops of cherry red liquid that were left in her cup.

I could see she was horrified. I got right in her face and snapped, "What the f*** are you doing pouring red crap into a cheap plastic cup for? If you spent a dollar and brought actual glassware with you, this wouldn't have happened! Damn it, you ruined my dress."

Trembling, the girl apologized and offered to pay for my dress. I barked, "You can't afford to pay for my dress!" I rushed down the bleacher stands and ran to the women's room. Donna followed behind. There was no way in hell I was going out into the middle of the field to stomp divots with a big red stain running down the back of my dress.

Donna continued to ramble in my ear about what an idiot the girl was. I nodded my head in agreement. "I can't go out on the field looking like this. People will laugh at me!" I told her.

Despite our attempts to remove it with cold water and soap, the stain was already set. And now it was soaked with water. Pissed, I said, "I'm leaving. I don't know how I'll get home, but I can't stay here looking like this. I want to kill that girl."

Desperate for me to stay, Donna said, "You can't leave, Paul is playing." That was true. I wanted to watch him play and get together with him and his friends after the match. So against every wet bone in my body, I stayed.

Returning to my seat, I told my friends we were moving. We abruptly got up, packed our picnic basket, threw one last glare at the group behind us, and moved several bleacher stands away. For the rest of the match, my friends and I bitched about what a pathetic group those "Pompano Beach" losers were.

Living in Boca gave birth to my bitch. I learned to be curt, nasty, and malicious. My bitch really came to life when I entered corporate America. Sure, I had studied and imitated the bitches in Boca, but even I never dreamed of who I would become and what I was capable of doing, given the opportunity.

Chapter 11

THE MAKING OF A CORPORATE BITCH

I admit, in both my personal and professional lives, being a bitch made things come much easier for me. Like the first time I had to fire someone who worked for me, or, *failed* to work for me.

One of my college mentors suggested I pursue a managerial position at one of the local department stores. Although I was quite young, I had considerable retail experience. He said it would give me access to easy advancement opportunities.

Armed with my resume, I marched into the human resources office of one of the largest, mid-range retailers in South Florida. Confident to the point of cocky, I stood with my shoulders back, chest out, and introduced myself to the receptionist in the office. I requested an interview on the spot. *Heck,* I thought, *Mr. Dunphy was right. I've worked at or managed three or four retail organizations since I was fourteen. I have more than enough experience to manage a department here!* And, I thought, *Who better to serve their Boca customers than a fellow bitch?*

My request for an interview was granted. After a series of meetings with various members of store management, I was hired as the department manager of the women's sportswear department.

Although I had never mastered chess, both my father and Mr. Maiocco, my favorite high school teacher, taught me a lesson I have never forgotten: *always think three steps ahead.* It was a huge lesson in planning, strategizing, and visioning, and it became a key strategy in my career. In fact, by the time I had my interview, I had already planned the next three steps which I knew for certain would lead me to the corporate hallways in Miami.

A few short months after being hired, I was promoted to a larger department, more critical to the store's overall success—lingerie. Immediately, I began strategizing, searching for ways I could use my new position to catch the attention of corporate management. I decided I would do this by turning my store's lingerie department into one of the highest-selling departments in the entire company.

In the 1980's, there was no effective system for reporting sales and inventory levels of a department within a store. Every sales tag was handwritten. In a department like lingerie, that meant hundreds of pairs of panties, bras, camisoles, and dusters. More important, if you intended to have sufficient inventory to ensure high sales volumes, you had to notify the corporate buyers of your inventory levels, as well as new trends your customers were looking for.

Fueled by my ambition to be the top-selling department in the corporate chain, I spent hours each morning drafting my own reports, by hand, of the inventory levels and sales results of each item in my department. I even included a trend report of fashion items that would build our sales volume. I decided to force the buyers and divisional manager into the store to meet me by burying them in paperwork and business analysis and impressing them with my determination to produce a great business. There was no way it could fail. I remembered what my high school business teacher, Mr. Maiocco, had taught me: *making money is all that matters to business. Make money for them and you will be rewarded.*

It worked! Before long, I was driving my very first car down the crazy highways of South Florida from Boca to Miami. Cars honked at me and drivers flipped me the bird as I taught myself to drive a stick shift on I-95.

I didn't care. They could give me the finger all they wanted. I was working in the corporate headquarters of a retail company where more promotions and opportunities awaited. I was so excited. I had already planned my next three steps. Next stop: Divisional Merchandise Manager (DMM). Overly-confident and bold, I shared my plans with my new DMM, Diana.

Diana was the epitome of class, intelligence, and ambition. Dressed every day to the nines, she was the embodiment of the advice my father had given me: *"Be properly dressed and you can get in anywhere."* Diana was so obsessed with appearance that if any of the buyers showed up at work with a torn stocking or chipped nail polish, she would march them four levels down to the women's department to replace it. That strictness and discipline served me well over the years.

Diana encouraged the dreams and ambitions of her team members, especially the young and aggressive ones like me. Because we were both career-driven and determined, I figured she saw a lot of herself in me. I took complete advantage of that.

I settled into my new role as assistant buyer. Before long, I noticed that my manager's purchases consistently ran over budget. Worse, her purchases far exceeded required inventory levels and projected sales, a recipe for disaster. Always thinking three steps ahead, I saw this as an opportunity to fix the issue, be the hero, and replace my manager when she got fired, a win-win for me.

Every night for a week, my manager, Donna, and I stayed late or met at her house. We reviewed every purchase order she had written or was in the process of writing so we could calculate our inventory position. As the confirmed purchase orders mounted into the millions, it was obviously not fixable, at least not without the help or knowledge of senior management. We would have to call and cancel orders from some of the top lingerie vendors in the country. Before long, phones would start ringing in the company president's office. I realized that not only was Donna's job at risk, but if I wasn't careful, mine would be, too. I thought, *I'll be damned if her mistakes are going to jeopardize my career. It just got started.*

I went over Donna's head and told Diana about the financial mess we were in. I alienated myself from Donna and made sure Diana knew that I was doing everything in my power to fix the mess and would do whatever she needed. "I am perfectly capable of getting these orders cancelled, Diana," I told her. I was covering my ass, and at the same time, opening up an opportunity for myself.

Moments after our meeting, Diana called Donna into her office and fired her. I re-emphasized my willingness to go to New York to negotiate our way out of the orders. "We'll, at least, minimize the markdowns we'll have to take from all of the overstock," I told her. Diana told the company president about our situation and plan.

A day or so later, our senior vice president asked me whether I had handled such negotiations before. "Absolutely!" I said, praying he wouldn't find out I actually had not. *How else do you get ahead?* I thought to myself.

"Great, then, go do it!" he replied, as he turned and walked away. I was off to New York that next week.

I placed a frantic call to my brother, Chris, who lived in New York. "Chris, I need a layout of Manhattan. I'm coming up next week."

"You need me to what?" he laughed.

"I'm coming to negotiate some merchandise cancellations and my vendor showrooms are scattered all around the city," I said. "I need you to tell me the best route to take to ensure I get to all of the meetings on time. I may even have the senior vice president traveling with me."

I gave him the address of each of the showrooms and he helped lay out a map. Manhattan was a grid, which made it easy. I carried that loose leaf map with me everywhere I went, hiding it from anyone traveling with me. After a couple of days of running up and down Madison Avenue, running in and out of showrooms, the cancellations were adding up. I was feeling great. There was definitely a promotion coming; I could feel it.

Even I was impressed with how well I navigated the city. Alternating between taxis and walking, I made my way through the city as if I had been there a hundred times. On the last day of our trip, the senior vice president said to me, "You know the city really well. Do you come here often?"

Laughing, I replied, "No. This is my first time."

"Really? You've never been here?" he asked, incredulous. "But you said you would have no problem coming to New York to handle these cancellations."

"That was true, I had no problem coming to New York," I agreed. "You never asked if I had ever been to New York." We both laughed.

"Very impressive. Good job", he said.

I wasn't formally promoted as I had hoped, but I did receive a salary increase. A couple of weeks later, my department merged with another. A few months after that, the company was bought out by another company. With my three-step plan and my 'bitch' gaining momentum, I moved on to conquer the next opportunity.

Chapter 12

CLAWING MY WAY TO THE TOP

Merchandising executives had noticed me on that New York trip, as well as during several other buying trips. Before long, comments began to circulate about the young woman who blew through showrooms, ripping up purchase orders, writing new ones, and running through the racks of samples to score future purchases.

For several weeks in 1985, a persistent executive recruiter hounded me to accept a position with another retailer in Miami. With fifty-one stores across Florida, the company was recruiting new talent to attract a younger customer base. According to the recruiter, there was a buying position open in lingerie, one of their largest divisions. I figured it could be another step up the corporate ladder and one step closer to my ambitious goal of running a major corporation myself.

Enticed by a big job with a big paycheck and plenty of big opportunities, I accepted the job and a few weeks later, was once again packing my belongings and heading toward bigger money, bigger position, and an even bigger ego trip.

My new job was with a fifty year-old department store headquartered in North Miami, twenty minutes closer to home. The retailer was a senior citizen's discounter. Long before Walmart and Target, it was the place to go for cheap, yet fashionable, clothing and house wares.

Feeling confident and cocky, I drove to work on my first day at the new company. I reached the offices in record time, ready to take on the world.

As I pulled into the parking lot at the front of the building, it was completely empty. *Where is everyone?* I thought. *It's already 7:00 a.m.* At my old company, the parking lot was full by 7:00 a.m. This was new territory for me, and there were definitely trails to be blazed. I checked my reflection in the rearview mirror one last time. I made sure that my brows were groomed, my make-up fresh, and my long, bleached blonde hair was smooth and in place. I looked over my nail polish to make sure it was chip-free and glanced down at my stockings to be sure they were run-free. I stepped out of the car and took one last glance in the side windows to check my suit and blouse. Buttons were fastened and zippers were up. I dabbed on a final layer of lipstick and was ready to go.

I had a distinctive corporate style; big hair, and a lot of make-up. I wore a colorful blouse and bright shoes every once in awhile, but most of my outfits were black, navy, or brown. They were tailored and starched and had little or no swing to them. I didn't want to appear too feminine, too soft. In the 80's, the trend for businesswomen was manly, and if the powerhouse women wore men's clothes, so did I. After all, the image of the powerful, corporate woman screamed, "bitch" and I was proud to fit the bill.

With my father's words, *Shoulders back, chest out, and head up,* running through my mind, I strutted through the parking lot. I threw open the front lobby door, whipped past the guard on duty, and headed straight down the long hallway. I was on a mission to find my new office and get my future moving. There was no time to waste.

The headquarters office was a large distribution center with an office building attached to the front of it. The building looked and smelled like it was more than a hundred years old. Working only from memory of my visit there a few weeks earlier, I wandered the hallways, trying to find the main office. I turned the final corner into the large, open office area of the merchandising division and realized I was the only person in the building. *People, it is after 7:00 a.m. Where are you?* I wondered. I walked up and down each of the hallways in the merchandising area, checking my colleagues' offices. I scanned pictures, framed certificates, and anything else that would give me a heads up on who I was working with, or more accurately competing against.

From the time I was very young, I found the silence of the mornings gave me time to catch up on work I had to finish or start, without interruptions. Now, as a manager, I used that time to strategize and plan my overall business, as well as my next career moves. Adding two hours to my workday not only allowed me to get my work done ahead of schedule, but also gave me great opportunities to take on new projects without interfering with my primary responsibilities. I was always moving one step closer to my money and power goals. That was my constant thought process—think and act three moves ahead.

I finally made my way to my new office. I was thrilled to see that the office was immaculate. My new desk was clutter-free, except for one piece of paper lying smack-dab in the center of it. From where I stood, I could make out that it was a cartoon.

I walked around to look down at the paper. It was a Garfield cartoon. *Oh good*, I thought, *someone left me a cute Garfield cartoon to welcome me. I love Garfield!* Upon closer examination, I realized it wasn't a welcome message. The cartoon had been placed there by someone who wasn't happy about my arrival. I picked up the cartoon and noticed it had been altered with white out; some of the original words were covered up. I couldn't make out the original words, but the message was clear.

The picture was of Garfield climbing a tree, long claws extended, and dark, zigzag claw marks under them. Looking back over his shoulder, he flashed an evil look, eyes full of deceit. The handwritten caption read, 'Clawing your way to the top'. *Ouch*, I thought. *Obviously someone doesn't like me and definitely doesn't want me here.*

I laughed and placed the cartoon back on the desk, positioning it so others could see it as they passed by. I was not going to hide it or hide from it. Like everything else, I would face it head on. *I could care less if someone's pissed that I got their job*, I thought. *If they wanted the position and didn't get it, that's not my issue, it's theirs. They should go to the decision maker(s) to find out why they passed him/her over.* Chuckling, I began looking over the binders of reports and drawers of files. There was no time to worry about someone I didn't know and who had no clue about me.

People began arriving around eight-thirty a.m. Buyers and assistants stopped by to check out the new girl, the one who possibly took their job. Some came in to introduce themselves with a big smile; others just shook my hand and told me their name, not "Hello," or "Welcome," and certainly not, "Good Luck." It was clear they didn't welcome outsiders and judging from most of their ages, hiring usually took place from within. I was an outsider. *Sucks for them*, I thought.

I soon discovered who had left the Garfield cartoon on my desk. It became evident what also might have fueled her anger. Here I was, an outsider in my early twenties, walking into a company whose average buyer was forty-plus, taking a job from someone who felt they deserved it based on their years of loyalty.

Over the next several weeks, the office gossip included everything from my being an outsider, to my sharing the Garfield cartoon, to 'the kid' who stole someone else's job. Snarls and virtual knives were thrown at my back non-stop. If any of them thought I was going to apologize for taking the job, they had another thing coming. I didn't apologize for anything.

If Boca was the home of the bitches, this company and division made up of all women was another breeding ground for them. I jumped right in to join and to learn from the best of them.

I learned why the parking lot was empty until eight or eight-thirty. The typical worker was over fifty; they didn't rush to get into the office. Claire, one of my assistants, was in her seventies. She wore slippers and a duster to the office. I was young, snappy, and curt, and I thought I could teach these folks a thing or two. As it turned out, these women, young and old, knew how to use their claws and used them often. If the Boca Bitches didn't completely influence my own bitch, these women all working together in close quarters certainly did.

Patricia was my first boss. She was a tall, domineering, and imposing woman in her forties. I admired her extensive knowledge of retail and merchandising, as well as her tenacity for getting the job done. I made it my mission for her to mentor me, teaching me the ropes of retail beyond buying and merchandising. Like Diana, I told her up front that I wanted her job and the position, power, and money that came with it. I'm not sure what she thought about that, but I didn't really care.

Patricia was a real bitch if you didn't make your numbers and she didn't care who knew it. When someone put her at risk of not delivering results, having to justify her actions to the executive offices, she would berate them so loud, you could hear her across the complex. First came the wind of her six-foot-plus frame storming out of her office and down the hallway to the guilty buyer's office. Then, her low, husky voice would rise as the discussion turned from argument to accusations and finger pointing. As the months went by, I realized that people obeyed her because of her stern disciplinary ways and take-no-prisoners approach. *Not all bad*, I thought.

However, Patricia fought for her team, no matter what the issue or how big the mess. She could berate her team, but wouldn't allow anyone else to. Those confusing, contradictory actions made me think that the balance of the two, bitch and defender, worked. I could be curt, backstabbing and ruthless, and at the same time, supportive and protective. Six months into my new job, a position opened that I knew would be perfect for me. Growing frustrated with Patricia's failure to promote me, I took it upon myself to go to the CEO to discuss it with him. *It's long overdue*, I thought, *and I deserve the promotion.*

The buyers in my division were shocked. "How dare she go over Patricia's head?" several of them commented behind my back.

"Who do you think you are going right up to his office demanding a promotion?" others inquired to my face.

"Because I can," I remarked snidely. That left them flabbergasted and me feeling empowered. I had earned and deserved the promotion. Besides, both Patricia and the CEO told me I would be promoted within months of coming into the company. I was simply calling in the debt. So off to the CEO's office I went.

The company was run like a family business, with open-door policies and no appointment necessary to see the CEO. A simple knock at the door was all it took to gain entry. I knew the CEO would open his door to me. We'd had a run-in just a few weeks earlier.

It was Monday morning and I was running late for my early morning planning. To make up time, I raced my Saab down I-95, winding in and out of cars, cutting off anyone who got in my way or slowed me down.

One of the cars was a red, convertible Corvette whose middle-aged driver cruised like he was out for a Sunday drive. I tried to get around him, but the ass decided to play cat and mouse with me. I jumped in front of him and he raced up behind me and rode my bumper, knowing I wouldn't hit the brakes. Then he jumped me, and I sped up faster to jump in front of him. It was becoming reckless.

He pulled out sharply to my right, raced out ahead, and jumped in front of me again. Pissed off, I raced alongside him, gave him a sideways glance, and gave him the finger, screaming, "Screw you!" I backed off the pedal and let him rip his Corvette past me and down the highway.

Blood pressure boiling, I took out my anger on the poor, defenseless drivers who remained on the road.

Still worked up when I got to the office, I had far too much work to do to waste the day worrying about the asshole in the red Corvette. I tackled the piles of reports on my desk, forgetting about the morning race. A couple hours later, I was standing at the copier in the main hallway printing my department's weekly reports. The CEO came shooting around the corner and stopped in his tracks when he saw me. With a devilish grin on his face, he said, "Did you realize that was me you flipped off this morning?"

Shocked, but without hesitation, I said, "Get out of the fast lane if you don't want to keep up!" Once I said it, I prayed he wouldn't fire me right there on the spot. *What balls I had to say this to the CEO*, I thought, beginning to sweat a little.

He burst out laughing. Relieved, I joined in with him. Without a word, he turned and walked away. For several months afterward, every time we saw each other, we would laugh. I was hoping for that same response today. I knocked on the CEO's door. "Come in!" he shouted.

Never the kiss-ass, diplomatic type, I cut past chit-chat and dove into the reason I was there. "I want to be interviewed for the open buyer position."

He didn't flinch, well aware of my ambition and that this position would give me the visibility, responsibility, and budget or 'big pencil' I wanted. He calmly replied, "Bernadette, you've only been here for six months. You should take more time."

"You're right, I have been here for six months, and that has been plenty of time to prove myself," I rebutted. "I have raised sales in the division and even increased our margins. I deserve this position more than anyone else out there." I remembered the backlash I received when I started my current job at the company. Although I didn't want to go through that shit again, I didn't care if someone else would be pissed; I deserved the promotion.

He mentioned that other buyers in the company were being considered. I retorted with a slew of insults against my competitors, like, "She can't negotiate prices to save her life," and, "Her fashion taste sucks; it's why there are such high markdowns in her department!" or, "None of them can handle the vendors and manufacturers like I can!"

"Bernadette, it's not your time," he said, calmly.

"What the hell does that mean?" I demanded.

"There's a right time and place for everything, and this isn't it," he stated, and that was that. I got up and went back to work and waited for the next opening.

Nearly twenty-five years later, I still remember his words. I don't always accept them, especially when I'm determined to get what I want. But when I look back on certain situations in my life, I realize his words were true. There is a right time and place for everything.

A couple of months later, I did get a promotion, exactly what I was looking for: visibility, greater responsibility, and a broader range of authority.

That promotion triggered an even fiercer, more arrogant bitchiness within me. It came with a much bigger sales quota, bigger office and that "bigger pencil," and a young whippersnapper of an assistant. I threw up my hands dramatically and cheered, "Finally, I'm done with old lady assistants!" Claire, my former, seventy year-old assistant, was seated at her desk when I said it.

I gave my new assistant hell. I made her answer my every beck and call, jump when I told her to, and do exactly as I said. My ego grew so large; I even demanded she answer my phone, "Ms. Boas' office". The bitch in me was in full gear and poor Renee was one more victim in the lineup that spanned many years.

My coworkers prematurely likened me to Garfield upon my arrival. By the time I left the company ten years later, I had more than earned the reputation as a catty, manipulative bitch who clawed my way to the top. Before I left, one man ensured the label, "bitch," was stamped in flames on my forehead forever. His name was Ben.

Chapter 13

THE MAN IN THE MIRROR

I could hear his voice five rows over from the corner office. "Bernadette! Get to my office. Now!" His voice bounced off the walls and cubicles between us. Ben was the ultimate bitch, a male bitch. If you put the two of us next to one another, you couldn't tell us apart, except that I was younger and a woman. We both had the same attitude, anger, and competitive personality that wreaked havoc on everyone around us.

Those who knew Ben would describe him as a bastard, but that seems too kind. Most often, when a man carries on like a bitchy woman, he is considered strong, courageous, a risk taker, or even 'ballsy'. He is never considered a bitch. But Ben? He was a bitch. And you can imagine what happens when two bitches are forced to work together on a daily basis; all hell breaks loose. The only saving grace was that I worked with Ben and not for him.

Ben brought out my inner bitch in a way that all of the Boca Bitches and catty women in Miami never could. I never intended to emulate him, but working with Ben sealed the deal that "bitch" became a permanent, accurate description of my personality.

Ben headed up the Business Reporting and Analytics Group. He thought and acted as if he were God. He wanted everyone to fear him and bow down to his every demand.

To most of us, he was Satan. We stayed far away from him to avoid being scorched. Judging by the venomous tone, with which he summoned me to his office, today was my day to be burned. Braced for a fight with the Dark Lord, I donned my bitchiest armor. Pissed that he was screaming for me from across the floor, I got up from my desk and stalked off to his office. Several of my colleagues stood up to watch my fiery descent into Satan's den. They taunted me, saying I was walking the plank to my fiery death. I simply turned to them and smiled.

There were times I actually enjoyed these confrontations with Ben. I looked at my interactions with him as competitions, negotiations, a game of cat and mouse that I was determined to win. Sometimes it was actually fun to play tit-for-tat with him. Other times, it tested every ounce of my self-control.

Ben was responsible for providing the merchandise reporting to the organization. He thought every one of the buyers was accountable to him for the inventory and respective markdown levels. Today, he was on the war path about some overstocked inventory or high markdowns. He was going to take it out on me, as if the lack of customers walking through the door was my fault.

When I reached his office, I slammed the door and stood in front of his desk, arms crossed, "Where do you get off yelling across the building for me? If you need me, come to my office and get me."

Ben sat still, back arched, arms outstretched and hands grasping the front of his desk, as if he was about to lunge at me. "I will call you any way I care to," he bellowed. "Where the hell do you get off ordering ten thousand panties, let alone thongs, for a one day sale? Are you crazy?" he barked.

Glaring back at him, I said, "Who the hell made you the buyer, Ben? I don't tell you how to run your business; don't even try to tell me how to run mine. Go take your crap out on someone else." With that, I turned and stomped out of his office, slamming the door behind me.

Granted, no one had ever taken such a risk on a new product like this one, thong panties for a senior citizens' discount retailer. Frederick's of Hollywood and a new, smaller lingerie store, Victoria's Secret, were taking the lingerie industry by storm. I was convinced that both the younger and older women of Florida were ready for something new and spicy. It was a risk I was willing to take, regardless of the backlash I sensed I would get. I certainly didn't care what Ben thought. *Who the hell was he to challenge my taste and knowledge of trends?* And the bet paid off, we sold thousands of the sexy string like thongs. That pissed off Ben even more.

I headed back to my office, ranting, "That man is a f*** lunatic!" The roar of laughter from behind the cubicles even made me laugh.

When I reached my office, I slammed and locked the door behind me, holding Renee hostage as I ranted for the next twenty minutes. "Who the f*** does he think he is?" I yelled. Renee was smart enough to sit there, nod her head in agreement, and let me go on. I would calm down eventually.

Ben came to the door thirty minutes later, knocking hard and yelling at me through the door to open up. "Go to hell, Ben!" I had Renee turn up the volume on her radio and we went on working. It was just another day with Ben.

Several months later, I was back in Ben's office arguing with him about Mothers Day results—or the lack thereof. Retail as a whole was taking a major hit that year, and lingerie was not protected by it. In the middle of one of our usual, insult-laden arguments, Ben pointed to the ceiling, at the frosted black half-globe that hung from it. "There are cameras in those lights," he began. "You pull your crap one more time with me, and I will show it to management."

Knowing he was full of crap and that his actions as a VP would be perceived much worse than mine, I called his bluff. "Go ahead; you do that, Ben," I snapped. "We will see who management thinks is off base."

He fell silent, pointed at the door, and ordered me out of his office. Smirking, I turned to leave. Then, I stopped, turned around, and grabbed one of the chairs that sat in front of his desk. I jumped up on it and pulled the globe from the ceiling fixture. There was no camera. Ben was making idle threats, expecting me to back down. He should have known me better.

I jumped down, dropped the globe onto the chair, turned and left his office without a word. *What an asshole,* I thought. That episode kept him quiet for awhile.

Then, as if God was mocking me or wanted to teach me a huge lesson, eight years into working for the company and dealing daily with Ben's raging moods, I ended up working for Satan, himself. And believe it or not, I actually asked for this privilege.

I had grown increasingly ambitious and impatient to obtain power, more money, and position. That impatience controlled me. Always thinking three moves ahead, I got bored quickly with the current job or project at hand. I would search out opportunities that would satisfy my boredom and advance my career. In many ways, I was an entrepreneur working for a corporate organization. Or, maybe an intrapreneur—someone possessing entrepreneurial traits and characteristics pursued and achieved within a corporate job. Throughout my career, my intrapreneurial spirit fueled me, helping me find and take on new challenges and risks. I loved it.

They allowed me to get my hands and sometimes, my reputation, dirty when I unearthed a business problem that wasn't being addressed. Once again, I found one and it was Ben's group that had the problem. *This ought to be good,* I said to myself, as I headed to the front office to discuss the opportunity with the CEO.

A buyer's primary responsibility is to analyze the daily business activities of each of a company's stores. He or she must know how sales product levels, markdowns, and the overall turn of inventory impact the profitability of the department. Ben's group was responsible for providing that reporting, but he lived in the stone age of paper. Reporting the buyers received was often a week or more late and buried in a 1,200-page flip report. In the newly competitive, computer-run marketplace, that just wouldn't do. We needed to get the reporting online, automated, and available to the merchants on a daily basis. "I'm the person for the job!" I told the CEO.

It was 1992 and the beautiful, black screen and green lettering of the desktop PC was picking up steam. Ben didn't understand what the PC meant to business analysis. I saw great risk to the company if we didn't catch up to our competitors. Ben never listened to what the buyers needed, only what he thought they needed. That was going to get us in trouble. I proposed a new department of business analysts working with both the buyers to discover their data and analysis needs and our IT department to implement online business intelligence reporting. The CEO loved the idea.

What I didn't expect was for our new Business Solution Support department to be set up within Ben's group. My bitchy personality became even more pronounced. My plan was to control and manage how this new group would be structured and operated. I would build it up as a significant part of the overall business. Merchandising and later the other departments would be completely dependent on my group. We would deliver what the business users wanted, eliminating the need for the existing analytical groups. Paper-run functions would be obsolete. Always thinking three moves ahead, once my plan was implemented, I wouldn't be working with Ben much longer. Eventually, he would be working for me. Within days of my promotion, I was putting that to the test.

I now had more than twenty employees reporting to me, and my ego was well-fed and prepared to take on Ben or anyone who got in my way. My new team, originally part of Satan's team, knew I had adopted his ways. My position definitely went to my head and everyone paid for it.

My first order of business was obtaining more office space to house my growing team. At the same time, I focused on securing my own office, a bigger one, to go along with my bigger job. I told Ben directly that I would be looking for an office for myself.

"You can share an office with one of the women," he said.

"I don't think so," I rebutted.

"There are no offices. Deal with it," he said.

He was right; there were no other solo offices, just open space cubicle offices in my team's work area. I was not having any of that. I wanted and would have my own office. *I was a department head after all*, I thought. I was not about to go backward and reduce my office size or anything else for that matter, Ben or no Ben.

Regardless of how petty or bitchy others thought I was, I was on a mission to find myself a new office.

To Ben's dismay, I found the perfect office. It was being used to store piles of reports and was packed from floor to ceiling with boxes of useless, outdated paper. *What a waste of space,* I thought. I told Ben I was going to have it cleared out.

"Absolutely not!" he objected.

"Just watch me," I promised, walking away, more determined than ever.

I went back to the bay of cubicles where my team sat. I pointed at four of them and said, "Come with me!" They hesitated. "Let's go!" I yelled. Nancy, Shirley, Tony, and Louise left their desks and scurried down the hall toward me.

Ben met me at the door, refusing to let me open it. "Ben, get the hell out of my way. There is no reason this room cannot be my office. Name one reason!" I demanded. Unable to, he angrily stormed off to his office and slammed the door.

I opened the door to the storage room, pointed to the stacks of paper, and said, "I need all these reports and boxes moved down the hall to the other storage room."

They poked their head into the room and asked, "Us?"

"Yes, you!" I demanded. "Why would I have called for you if I didn't want you to do it?"

Nancy balked and under her breath said, "No way!"

"What did you say?" I challenged.

"Nothing!" she replied.

"I thought so. Now get to it, and let me know when you're done." I turned around and went back down the hall to my temporary office.

As they moved boxes from one office to another, my new employees complained. Their hateful remarks floated down the hallway to my office. After all, I had just become their boss and was already having them drag boxes of paper down a hallway to another office, just so I could have my own office. *I am not taking an office that was meant for one of my analysts. They'll just have to deal with it,* I reasoned.

"Quit complaining and just get it done!" I shouted. Ben just sat in his office, glaring at me every time I passed him.

Through the years I never paid attention to the *"what goes around comes around"* karma. I didn't believe it applied to me. So what if I was a bitch? It was working for me, and no one was stopping me, not even Ben. But when I left Ben, the company, and Boca for what I thought was the last time, I realized that God had other plans for me. The time had come to pay the piper.

Chapter 14

THE SUPERWOMAN SYNDROME

By my early thirties, my bitchiness was fully ingrained into who I was. Looking into the mirror, the scowl across my face, the attitude in my strut, and the razor-sharp knife that was my tongue defined who I was to everyone who knew me.

Ambition not only defined, but consumed me. How could it not? I worked endless hours, took on several multiple, high-risk projects, and became the stereotypical, cut-throat, corporate bitch. I wanted it all and was so busy mastering this new way of living, I was blind to what it was doing to me emotionally, physically, and spiritually.

Physically, I was fit, lean, and strong. I was obsessed with working out and looking great. The idea of not working out made me go through withdrawals, both physically and mentally. I loved the feeling of sweat pouring down my face and arms and the exhaustion that left me gasping for breath after a long run or even a short bout with weights. I loved competing with both women and men on strength and endurance. I would always out lift or out run them. My legs were so strong, it was scary. I loved the deep night's sleep that followed a heavy workout. It helped me jump out of bed each morning, refreshed and ready to do it all over again. I felt powerful, indestructible, and practically immortal.

My mind was just as strong, or so I thought.

Despite my long hours and business travel, I still made time for friends, even if it was only on Friday nights. No matter where I was flying in from, or what was bogging me down at work, on Fridays at five o'clock, I headed to the local, trendy happy hour to catch up with friends.

We would down martinis and Jack Daniels and indulge our love of people watching. No place was good enough for us; *we* were too good for *them*, as servers and patrons would learn once we arrived. Dolled up in our little black dresses or spandex leggings and sexy tops with spiky, high heels, we acted like we were walking the red carpet at the Grammy's. We thought we were rock stars and wanted everyone else to think so, too.

I would hit the bar for my traditional vodka on the rocks, forcing my way between the two men or women who stood at the bar gabbing it up. "Do you mind?" I snapped at one of the girls, who couldn't have been more than nineteen or twenty.

"What the hell?" she snapped back at me.

"If you don't mind," I replied, squeezing myself between her and her friend, forcing my way to the bar counter.

"F*** you, lady!" the young girl blurted.

"Excuse me?" I replied. "Trust me, girlie, you do not want to go there. I might have to prove that you aren't even legal to be here!"

She made room for me to belly up to the bar to order a drink. I heard her whisper, "Bitch."

"Ouch," I laughed. "That hurt."

I snapped my fingers at the bartender, with his red, floral, Bahama shirt and long, straggly hair, to get his attention and order my drink. I threw a couple of dollars on the bar and turned to leave. But not just yet. I had to throw the young bitch another smirk. I had no idea what her boyfriend thought of me, nor did I care.

I never dated much in my twenties, at least not in the traditional sense. It was much easier to sleep with a guy or find one who lived some distance away and date him for several months. After all, there were no men in Boca.

They were married, gay, or emotionally detached. At least, that's what I told myself. How else could I explain my empty calendar? I never considered it had anything to do with the hard-ass attitude I presented to any man who approached me. Like the guy at an Atlanta sports bar who came up to me and my girlfriends one night.

It was one of our Friday happy hours. We gathered after work to shoot pool, grab a couple of beers, and meet some guys. At least, Holly, Lisa, and Ashley would. They showed up in their tight jeans and low-cut blouses, while I ended up coming right from work in my typical, high-neck blouse and suit pants. My big hair reached for the stars and my earrings could have been used for billiard balls.

We met three guys who were cute and definitely interested. My girlfriends were happy to oblige. I even considered it, until one guy turned to Lisa and whispered, "What's with the rich chick?"

What? I screamed internally. "Excuse me," I snapped.

Shocked that I had heard him, he stood up straight, pushed his chest out, and said, "You must be the rich chick of the group. That's a compliment."

"Really. That's a compliment," I retorted. "How stupid do you think I am? Be a man, and tell me what you really meant."

My friends were laughing. "Shut up!" I barked. I turned to the guy and demanded, "Well?"

He didn't hold back. "You're all dolled-up as if you're going to the theatre. You haven't said a word the entire time. You just watch with your nose turned up." he said. "I figured you're a rich snob or just an uptight bitch."

Ouch. Now, that did sting, but I wouldn't let him know that. Instead, I replied simply, "You're an asshole!"

"Hey, you asked," he said. I turned around, pissed, and went to the bar for a drink.

In my mind, I was in complete control of my life. If people saw me as something like a rich snob or bitch, it was their screwed-up perception, not mine. Despite my age, I still had not learned that perception is reality. I attributed people's perceptions of me to their own sorry lives. The way I saw it, the bitch that had taken hold was not sending me over the edge or tearing me down emotionally, spiritually, or physically. I was just fine. I was who I was, like it or not.

I used every possible excuse to justify why my phone didn't ring. *They're intimidated. I make too much money for him. He has his own emotional problems,* or, *he doesn't want to ruin the friendship.* I told myself anything and everything that would console me.

My friend, Sheila, who was unemotional, yet codependent, gave me the book, *He's Just Not That Into You,* by Greg Behrendt and Liz Tuccillo, as a gift. The authors argue that women make every excuse possible to justify why a man is not calling or asking them out. The hard truth, the authors write, is that women need to realize when a man is just not that in to them and move on.

"Did you get a copy for yourself, Sheila?" I snipped, when she handed me the book. *Who cares what the book says anyway?* I thought.

I prayed a lot in those days. It was all I had left after storming out of church one Easter Sunday while I was still in college. On that day, during one of the most religious celebrations of the year, the priest presiding over the congregation had the nerve to preach from the altar, "If you do not give every penny in your pocket to God, you are not a Christian." His words shook me to the core.

I was suddenly alert and poised for a fight. I wanted to storm from my seat and tackle him, not caring that he was a priest. A priest, whom I had admired and respected since arriving in Boca. In fact, I had been raised to respect all priests, cardinals, and bishops. That's why I didn't mind having to bow down in front of them and kiss their rings. Yet, here was this priest accusing me of not being a Christian.

Not caring that I was in a pew toward the front altar, or that the priest was in the middle of his homily, I stood up, glared at him, and stormed down the aisle and out the back door of the church. As I slammed open the doors, the sun shone on the church walls. It would take seven years and the death of one of my best friends, Sid, to get me to go back.

During my hiatus from the church, I made my own connection with the Man above, in prayer. With all of my carrying on and the precarious situations I was putting myself in, that one-on-one time was critical. As much as I still saw myself as the same '5-F' girl I always was, everyone and everything around me challenged that belief. Even my family and friends could see I was no longer the same sassy and precocious person I had been. It's too bad I was too self-absorbed to notice the subtle ways they were trying to let me know.

In my late twenties, my oldest sister, Mary, gave me the book, *The Superwoman Syndrome,* by Marjorie Hansen Shaevitz. The book speaks about women trying to have it all—family, career, and money. It discussed how women were jeopardizing their relationships and their lives in their pursuit. They were risking themselves physically with stress; heart attacks in women were on the rise and divorce rates rose drastically as they tried to create a life that included both a career and family. The feminist movement of the 60's and 70's had thrown open so many doors and windows of opportunity for women that trying to tackle them all often created anxiety and stress, jeopardizing their health. *What does this have to do with me?* I remember thinking. *I have no husband, kids, or PTA meetings to attend. What is she thinking?*

Looking in the mirror, all I saw was a young woman doing it all—climbing the corporate ladder, burning the candle at both ends, and playing the game very well. I wasn't making any sacrifice; I was pursuing the best things life had to offer. To me, that had nothing to do with being a superwoman, though it was cool to think about. *Heck, I'd love to be her,* I thought. *And if I could wear her tight leotards, shorts, spiked heels and fly that would be even better.*

But that wasn't me. All I had was my ambition for money, position, and power. No husband, no relationship, no children, not even a pet at the time. I loved being single, having money, and the power to do what I wanted, when I wanted, with whom I wanted, regardless of the cost. If other people were envious of me, it was for that reason, and I took full advantage of it.

Still, I struggled to understand Mary's intention for giving me the book, without coming right out and asking her. I thought, *Maybe this is her warning to me that if I continue on this path, I'll never have the husband or kids I've always wanted.* I recalled a conversation I had a few years earlier with my sister, Peggy.

On a trip home to Philadelphia to visit the family, I met up with Peggy at her downtown apartment. Peggy has always been my confidante and sounding board on life issues, men, and business. This particular evening, I was raving about the most recent promotion I had earned at work. I bragged about the salary increase, my move to a luxury apartment, and my new car. I told her about the large team I was now heading up, the visibility with management, and raved about the opportunity for travel. Peggy listened, smiled, and nodded her head as if in agreement. When I finally shut up, she said something I have never forgotten.

"I'm just worried, Bernadette, that your ambitions and focus on your career and money will prevent you from ever getting married or having kids." *F****, I thought. Why is she throwing up all over my great news? What the hell does she mean I will never get married or have kids?* As much as I felt like smacking her, I really wanted to crawl under her couch and hide.

I chuckled in an attempt to cover up the feeling of uncertainty and insecurity that stirred inside me. "Peggy, there is plenty of time for a husband and kids; I'm not even thirty," I said. I felt a knot in my stomach and pressure in my neck. My head was swirling. Pursuing promotions and material things was so much easier, so much more rewarding than the dating scene. It was certainly less painful.

From my early twenties through my forties, I wrestled with a neurosis, a "fear of missing out on anything and everything," or what I called my FMOAE. Having lived in Boca, a city of wannabe's, I quickly became addicted to wanting anything and everything. That included the latest shoes, pocketbooks, or clothes, the best parties, nightclubs, and restaurants. It even included the latest, slickest cars and even the first "brick" cell phone. For a time, it even included the hottest new guy in town, even if he was only looking for a one-night stand.

If I were to describe myself and how I walked through life for so many years, it would be desperate, anxious, hyper, paranoid, and determined to be where the beautiful people were. I would race, clamor, and even claw my way to whatever was going on because if it went on without me, I would physically ache and believe I was losing everything. The world would stop turning if I missed out on something, even when I had no idea what that "something" was. At times, I would get so worked up that I became panic-stricken. That is where my bitch would really shine, and it happened more often than anyone could guess.

I remember a big charity event, a casino night, going on at the Boca Hotel. It was the event of the season and I wasn't about to miss it. I brought my little black dress and heels to work so I could change and go straight to the hotel. I didn't want to miss the big announcement, the arrival of the best-looking guy, or the free drinks and hors d'oeuvres. *God knows,* I thought, *if I'm even ten minutes late, it will all be gone.*

I headed up I-95 long before rush hour set in. Just north of Fort Lauderdale, the highway came to a crawl, then to a complete stop. Not sure what had caused the delay, I sat in my car stewing, then steaming, then yelling, as if that would magically clear a major accident miles up the road.

My heart began to race so fast, I thought I was having a heart attack right there on the highway. I just knew I was going to miss something spectacular. It was physically debilitating and mentally exhausting.

I had no clue what others thought of my neurosis. If people who knew me at that time were to label me as anything; it would have to be obsessive-compulsive. Compulsions, both personal and professional, controlled me.

I worked out seven days a week, often many times a day. I would run despite a twisted ankle or a 105-degree fever. I went out night after night, smoking, drinking, and carrying on, afraid that if I didn't, something unbelievable would happen without me. When it came to drinking or eating, at times, once I started, I didn't stop. Not because I needed it, but because it was there, and if I didn't have it, I didn't want anyone else to, either. It all started over a box of cereal when I was a young girl.

In our family of fourteen, we lacked nothing. Although my parents watched their pennies, serving us 'shit on a shingle'—corned beef, cream and toast in warm milk—they also spoiled us with camping trips, vacations to Disney World, summer trips to the shore, and so much more. One of their splurges was sugared cereal.

Each week for many years, 7-Eleven and other grocery stores and restaurants delivered enough gallons of milk, tubs of condiments, and loaves of bread to feed our large family. On random occasions, my mother would splurge and buy our favorite ice cream and sugared cereal—Cap'n Crunch, Honey Combs, or Lucky Charms. In our house, with six boys and my father, food didn't last long, especially 'special' food like sugared cereal.

When Mom wasn't able to get into the house and hide those special purchases, we would see where she stashed them. Sometimes one of us would move them to a different spot so the others couldn't find them. After everyone went to sleep, I would sneak to the kitchen in the middle of the night and gorge, leaving only crumbs for the others. I figured that if I didn't eat it then, I would never get to, thanks to my growing brothers.

Even today, more than thirty years later, I can only bring single-size portions of snacks, meals, or beverages into my house. If I buy the regular size of anything, my FMOAE will taunt me until I finish the last gallon of ice cream, the large bag of Frito's, or box of sugared cereal. After all these years, I still have an all-or-nothing attitude. That's great in a competition or in a commitment, but it can wreak havoc on your emotional and physical state.

My compulsion to be part of anything and everything took hold and fueled the bitch in me as I reached my twenties and thirties. Call it the 'Superwoman Syndrome' or whatever you will. At that time, I didn't have the desire for the white picket fence with the tall, dark, handsome man and two beautiful children standing outside our colonial stone home in the suburbs. My superwoman complex had me beating down every other man and woman for the biggest corner office and the Rolex watch.

Chapter 15

LOSING MY HAIR

My ability to stay on track with my life plans, goals, and ambitions was derailed each and every morning I had to show up at work to deal with Ben. Things weren't getting easier between the two of us and it was not looking like it was going to change. I never imagined it could get worse, especially with hundreds of miles between us.

Several years before leaving Boca, I was putting myself in precarious situations not only professionally, but personally and physically, as well. If there was ever a doubt that my FMOAE neurosis was in full swing, the end of an evening out with friends confirmed it.

A couple of girlfriends and I headed to Guppy's restaurant in Boca to celebrate my recent promotion. My promotion not only gave me an ego boost, but it had me feeling pretty friendly on this particular night. A few of the rowdy guys standing at the bar noticed us the moment we walked in and decided to test how friendly I was.

I ordered my vodka on the rocks, gave a flirty smile to both Mike, the bartender, and the guys across the way and joined the girls at the other end of the bar. I could feel their eyes following my ass, and sensed one or two of them walking behind me. My friend, Sally, smirked at me and bobbed her head slightly to the right. I turned around to find one of them standing right behind me. I smiled, said hello, and offered a handshake. Instead of shaking my hand, he grabbed it and yanked me up against him. I jerked my arm free and backed away from him.

"What the hell do you think you're doing?" I yelled.

"Oh come on, babe, don't be like that!" he said, pulling me toward him again. "Let's have some fun!" he said, as he wrapped his arm around my waist and pulled my body up against him and his balls, hard.

Realizing very quickly that my innocent flirting was about to get me into some serious trouble, I barked, "Look, asshole, back off!" With all of my strength, I pushed him as hard as I could a couple of feet back and he hit the wall behind him. Before I could move away, he lunged at me with an extended fist. I stood there, frozen. In my head I was screaming, *Oh shit! What the hell!*

As he lunged at me, another fist, a much larger one, blocked his from slamming into my face. I was petrified. I glanced up to see Zac, a Guppy regular, grab the guy by the shirt and throw him down the aisle. "Get the hell out of this bar or you will find your ass in jail," Zac warned.

Standing there, my mouth gaped and heart racing, all I could think was, *Oh my God, that guy could have killed me. How the hell did I get myself into this?*

I was pissed off and shaken. All I was doing was flirting a little bit—a simple God damn smile, and this asshole decided that gave him the right to man handle me. *What a f***,* I thought. I hadn't planned to pick him up or any other guy up that night. I was just in such a great mood and wanted to use that ego boost to help me overcome my insecurities with men. *Was that so wrong?* I wondered.

No matter how sociable, daring, or engaging I was, I have felt insecure and afraid, of how boys/men would interpret my flirtations. So I didn't tend to flirt.

Maybe it began when I was ten and woke to some kid fondling me under my blanket at summer camp. Or when I was eleven having men and boys taunt me about my size 36C chest. It could have been the rejection and hurt I felt at age thirteen when my first boyfriend took back the ring he'd given me, threw it to the ground, and stomped on it in front of all our friends.

Maybe it was when John from Atlantic City stalked me after some innocent pecking and fondling. Steve H. didn't help any; when he called me a prude from across the room, at a tenth grade party, because I wouldn't go upstairs to screw around with him.

Those memories lingered, urging me to put up impenetrable walls very few guys could knock down. More often than not, innocent or purposeful flirtation led to unhappy endings. I decided to avoid these hurtful situations by not pursuing men, no matter how much I wanted to, with the exception of one-night stands or long-distance relationships. It was easier to be alone than take risks when it came to men.

"Are you all right?" Zac asked, wrapping his arm around my back to console me. Debbie was whispering something in my ear. I could see her mouth moving, but didn't hear a word.

My voice was shaking, "I am now. I'm so happy you were here, Zac. Thank you."

"I am too," he said, and turned to the bar to order a drink. I sighed and sat down on the bench against the wall.

Everyone knew not to mess with Zac, a local police officer. At 6'2" and two-hundred pounds, he was all muscle and considered a brut. Off-duty or on, Zac didn't tolerate drunks in this or any bar, which worked out beautifully for me that night.

As the night wore on, Zac ended up having too much to drink, throwing back all the free drinks folks passed him for coming to my rescue. No one gave a second thought to the fact that he was a cop.

By the time we decided to leave, he was too drunk to drive himself home. I offered to give him a ride. "It's the least I can do," I told Debbie and Sally. It wasn't easy to convince him to leave his car, and even harder to convince him that, although he was a cop, he wasn't above getting a DUI.

"You should know better Zac," I said. "You don't need to get pulled over—cop or no cop." He finally accepted.

Slumped over in the front seat, he mumbled flirtatious comments to me. Knowing he was drunk, I didn't pay any attention. By the time we reached his condo, I needed to use the bathroom and asked if I could come in. "Of course," he said. I expected him to drop onto his couch and pass out. I scurried quickly through the darkness to find his bathroom and shut the door behind me and collapsed onto the toilet. The drama of the evening came back to me. *I can't believe that guy was about to punch me*, I thought, beating myself up for being so careless. *Did I deserve his aggressiveness? Absolutely not! This was definitely not my fault.*

I splashed water on my face, walked out of the bathroom, and headed for the door. Making my way through the dark living room, I found Zac lying on the ground with his pants off.

"Zac, what the hell are you doing?"

"Oh, come on, Bernadette, I helped you earlier. Now you can help me," he pleaded, as he grabbed my arm and pulled me down to the floor on top of him. *What the f***?* I thought.

"Let go of me Zac. I already helped you by driving you home." I tried to pry my arms from his hold but couldn't. He turned over and was on top of me, his hands up my skirt pulling at my panties.

"Zac, what the f*** are you doing?" I yelled, struggling to free myself.

"Come on, Bernadette, I just want a little something," he pleaded.

How the hell do I get myself into these situations? I thought. The *guy at the bar got violent when I became aggressive. He lashed out because I lashed out. If I do the same thing now, there's a good chance the same thing will happen. I need to stay calm if I want to get myself out of here*, I thought. Zac was a cop. If he took this where it appeared to be going, it would be his word against mine.

"Zac," I said as I tried to pull his arm away. It didn't work. The next thing I knew, my skirt was up and my panties were off.

"Bernadette, come on," he pleaded again, maneuvering himself between my legs.

Panicked, I thought of the only thing I could do to get him off of me. I decided to sweet talk him, lie and tell him I wanted him, too, but not like this. *It was worth a shot*, I figured.

"Zac, this isn't the way you want this to happen, is it?" I whispered in his ear. "I want you, too, but not like this." He made it difficult to say anything as he pressed his open mouth on top of mine. He continued to force my legs open while I pressed my knees together with every ounce of strength I had.

"What do you mean?" he asked, excitedly. He lifted his head and looked down, the stench of beer on his breath.

"I'm not about to ever go out with you if you keep this up," I replied. "I know you've wanted to ask me out, but there is no way in hell that will ever happen."

He rolled off me and collapsed onto the floor. I looked over at him laying there, his full erection pointing to the ceiling. I took a deep breath and silently thanked God. I jumped up off the floor, desperate to get away, but he grabbed my hand and pulled me down onto the floor again. I firmly told him, "Zac, let go of me now. This is not going to happen. I'm going to put my panties back on. Put yours on, too?"

"But I'm not done yet!" he said. "Give me a blow job?" he begged, yanking me toward him.

Oh my God, I thought, *this is never going to end*. My initial instinct was to punch the shit out of him, like my mother did to those bullies. But having lived through knives being pulled on me and other men forcing me to have sex with them, I knew my bitch response wouldn't get me out of his house. I reached out and put his hand on his penis.

"Take care of yourself, Zac. That way, we're still good, right?"

Surprisingly, he looked at me and agreed, with a drunken slur, "Right."

As he got lost in his own pleasure, I got up, grabbed my purse, and made a bee line for the door. Once out of his house, I raced to the car. I got in behind the wheel and tore up my tires getting away from his condo as fast as I could. *Shit, I left my panties,* I thought.

I pulled out onto the main road, but couldn't focus enough to remap the route we had taken. I pulled over and frantically called Debbie. "Please, please, please be there", I cried out loud, tears streaming down my face. Thankfully, she answered. Frantic herself from the panic in my voice, she nonetheless talked me down Indian Trail Road, remaining on the phone until I was safely inside my apartment with the door locked.

For the next several months, any guy who even attempted to smile at me received a verbal whipping. "Wipe that smart ass smile off of your face, now!" I would snap. If my love life was suffering a slow patch before that night it soon experienced a drought. I was not going through that ever again.

"All guys are not like that asshole," Debbie tried to reassure me. Even though I knew she was right, my head kept screaming, *Block, shield, protect!*

Fourteen years in Boca, ten years with my company, and too many years of mastering a bitchy attitude to mask fears, insecurities, and feelings of unworthiness had led me to this point. *Something has to give,* I thought. *Something has to change.* I still didn't see that the change that was needed was within me. As hard as I tried to ignore it, I knew there had to be a message in the events of the evening. So many times in my life, there had been 'God's speaking' moments, to teach or prepare me for something. The fact that I was already telling myself things had to change meant God had something to tell me too.

I didn't want to hear it. I just wanted to go home to the security of my family. All I wanted was a big hug from my mother, an intelligent conversation with my father, and a tearful breakdown with my sister, Peggy.

No matter what I was going through, my family always gave me the most comfort. It was my sister, Peggy, who would call me out when I deserved it. I needed her to be straight with me, and I prayed for the strength to listen this time.

The weekend after that hellacious night, in August of 1994, I boarded a flight from Fort Lauderdale to Philadelphia. It was Britt's birthday, and my family had planned a gathering to celebrate. I was excited to see everyone, but I never thought my visit would be life-changing for me.

The morning of my trip, I raced around my apartment trying to find a specific pair of sandals. Drained and exhausted, I had slept through my alarm and was running late for the flight. Desperate to get out of town for a few days, I tore apart the couch, chairs, and closet looking for the sandals. Suddenly, I remembered taking them off in my car a day or so earlier at the gym. I closed up my bag and sprinted to the car.

Fort Lauderdale's airport can be hell to get through when you're late. I drove like Mario Andretti through the parking lot and tore through the airport like OJ Simpson. I reached my gate with ten minutes to spare.

Sweat pouring down my face, I collapsed into a seat next to an elderly couple and let out a long sigh.

"Are you okay, sweetie?" the elderly woman asked. I broke down in tears. "Oh, honey, everything is going to be okay. I promise," she said as her husband handed me his handkerchief.

"I'm fine, thank you. Just missing my family," I sobbed.

While that was true, it wasn't the whole story. I closed my eyes, and took a deep breath, reflecting on the last several months and years. *I have to do something*, I thought to myself. *Something's gotta give.* I needed to go home!

I wished the elderly couple a safe trip and boarded the plane at the first class seating announcement. Making my way to my seat, I pulled my ear plugs and eye mask from my bag, stowed everything else overhead, and sank into the window seat, looking forward to a much needed, two-hour nap. *Don't come over here,* I said to myself, when a flight attendant with a fake smile walked in my direction. I just wanted to be home in Philadelphia. The faster she could tend to the slow-moving passengers, unaccustomed to traveling, and get them out of the aisles and into their seats, the sooner we could get this plane up in the air heading north.

Traveling back and forth across the country over the years, I had adapted very well to sleeping on flights. It was my chance to escape from everything bearing down on me. With ear plugs in and eye mask on, I would fall asleep as soon as the wheels went up. Only when I felt the wheels come down or realized I was sleeping on my neighbor's shoulder, would I wake up.

This flight was no different. Exhausted by the hours spent dealing with Satan at work, hanging out with friends, and the terrifying night with Zac, I was sure sleep would come easy.

But God had different plans.

Three-quarters of the way into the flight, I was still wide awake, staring at the blackness behind my eye mask. Close to tears and desperate for sleep, I could see, feel, and hear everything—the babies crying, the drink cart slamming into the aisle seats, and the overweight couple bickering.

I gave up on sleep and stared aimlessly out the small window at the soothing blue sky. Sunlight glowed on the horizon, creating mountains of orange-laced clouds. The turquoise sky matched the jelly shoes I was wearing. The remaining pallet of yellow, orange, grey, and blue matched my Capri pants. It was breathtaking. I imagined the sky as a magnificent Monet painting, created by the clouds, as the colors brushed up against the plane and scattered in the wind.

I closed my eyes and listened to my own steady breathing, allowing the beauty in front of me to soak up my anxiety. The wheels dropped from the bottom of the plane. We were about to land in Atlanta. *Finally, halfway to Philadelphia,* I closed my eyes for the last twenty minutes of the flight, only to be startled by the final announcements blaring from the intercom above my head. It was obvious that sleep was not in the cards. I went back to staring out the window.

As the plane descended, mountains, trees, and green fields came into view. It was beautiful, and a far cry from the miles and miles of road, condos, and beaches of South Florida. All the times I had flown into and out of Atlanta, I had never noticed how beautiful Georgia was.

The plane made a sharp turn, pointing us eastbound and the Atlanta skyline was in full view. It was magnificent. I had grown to hate the South Florida skyline, as it represented the constant pursuit of what I wanted and didn't yet have. It was the people and things fighting and competing with me, and those that just wouldn't get out of my way.

I could see the runway. I felt excited and exhilarated. I was having one of my, "God's speaking" moments, and this time I was determined to stop, listen, and really feel His message. *Okay God, let me know what it is you want me to hear. I'm listening.* I closed my eyes, took a deep breath, and sat still. Instantly I said out loud, "I'll be living here a year from today," startling my neighbors and me. They looked at me like I was a little crazy. All I could do was smile.

As the plane taxied slowly to the gate in Philadelphia, my new life in Atlanta became my focus. I was ready to shout it out to Peggy and the rest of my family. Squirming in my seat, ready to jump up the minute the bell went 'ding,' the plane came to a complete stop. *What the hell! I thought.* For ten minutes, we sat without a word from the cockpit. I pushed the overhead call button. No one responded. Now, I was pissed. I wanted to get off the plane so I could tell my family about my plans. Finally, the plane's engine revved and we made our way to the gate. The crew never said a word to explain our delay. "Idiots," I commented to the man sitting next to me.

As I departed from the plane, I couldn't help but snap a rude comment to the attendants standing at the door. "Is it that hard to take five seconds to alert us as to why we are being inconvenienced?" They raised their eye brows and didn't say a word. I shook my head and walked off the plane.

Over the next couple days, I found myself laughing and crying with my family. Reliving the night with Zac was not easy; in fact, it was embarrassing. Sitting on the lower level of the snack bar at our local swim club, surrounded by bushes and trees, I talked and cried while Peggy listened, never judging me, but growing increasingly angry at the events of that evening and the pain they had caused me.

From the moment I walked into the house, my father knew something had happened to me. I gave him a hug and a kiss, but wasn't in the mood to talk. I certainly didn't want to hear his usual, "So babe, how's your love life?" Although he meant well, I was afraid I would break down in tears if he asked. So I avoided him. He knew something was wrong.

When Peggy and I returned to the group, my father reached out to take my hand and gently asked, "Are you okay, babe?" I wanted to fall into his lap and cry.

"I am now, Dad. Thanks," I said, my voice still a little shaky. I turned and quickly walked away toward the pool to join the kids. I could feel his concerned eyes following me. I imagined his heart sinking at the sight of one of his children, his seventh son, hurting.

When I returned to South Florida, the Fort Lauderdale skyline no longer bothered me. I had a new plan that didn't include Boca or Miami. By Monday morning, my plan to put my 'God's speaking' moment into motion was in full gear. I would ask for a transfer to our sister store headquarters in Atlanta, obviously, with a promotion. I had already begun searching for the best places to live and scoped out the social scene. Within two days of my 'God's speaking' moment, I had already mapped out my great escape.

I went directly to our new president to tell him I wanted to transfer to Atlanta.

"Why?" he asked.

"As you know, I've been working with the business solution support team there. They would greatly benefit from my being part of their immediate team to get these projects deployed," I said.

"But that doesn't explain why," he pressed.

"For a lot of reasons I don't want to talk about," I said.

"Do you at least know if they have a position open?" he asked.

I didn't know if they had an open position, but I did know they needed me. In the year or so I had been working with the group in Atlanta, I had developed a reputation for being difficult, demanding, curt, and impatient. Despite this, I knew they would welcome me. They needed me. I was the key to getting their projects done on time. Working side by side with them would be a win-win for everyone. I knew it and so did they.

"No, I don't know if they have a position," I said. "But they need me, and I doubt they'll say no," I surmised, arrogantly.

Whether he championed my goals, or was just happy at the prospect of my leaving, the president said he would support me. I was thrilled, Ben was ecstatic, and more than a few of my team members weren't too disappointed either.

My transfer was approved and several months later, I packed fourteen years into suitcases and boxes and drove north to my new life in Atlanta. *Adios Boca*, I thought. *If I never see your beautiful palm tree lined streets again, it will be too soon.*

Oh, how Murphy loves to taunt me.

I remember it like it was yesterday. Not because it was January 29, my birthday, but because it was the day a whole new level of bitch took over, one that would ultimately wreak havoc on everyone in my life.

It was in the first week at my new job in Atlanta. People were gossiping throughout the office. Everyone was freaked out about a big announcement expected to come down from management. I paid no attention to it. Speculation about a merger between the Atlanta and Miami offices had circulated since I'd joined the company ten years before.

Within minutes, managers circulated around the main office floor, telling everyone to head to the conference room for an announcement. Anxious and excited, we scurried to the second floor meeting room. Most people raced for the front row seats; I stood in the back, figuring I could best be seen by the CEO and his team, who would be standing up front.

The company's top executives walked in and stood in a straight line at the front of the room. They looked as if they were part of a police lineup, except they were smiling.

"We're merging with Miami," the president announced. "It will take six to nine months to complete the merger."

I was stunned and sad, but at the same time excited about what this could mean for me. I glanced at my new boss, Barbara, and shrugged my shoulders as if to say, *What now?* She threw me a look that read, *Who knows?*

What we did know was we were the Business Solution Support Group; responsible for all data the company used to run their business. The purpose of my Atlanta trips had been to create online analytics for all the sister companies within the organization. This gave both the parent company and the divisional companies the daily sales and margin results from each of the different store chains within the system, including Miami and now Atlanta.

Moving over closer to Barbara, I whispered, "We'll have to have input in this merger."

Knowing how greedy I was for title and recognition, she simply said, "Let's just wait and see, okay?"

"Sure!" I said, and went back to listen to the rest of the announcement.

The president began to announce the team of business users, technical, and systems folks who would be involved in making this merger happen. *I definitely want a role in this,* I thought, *and a big one at that. This could be huge for me if I play my cards right,* I said to myself, growing more and more excited.

Then, I heard the words, "The person to head up the systems and data conversion of this merger will be Bernadette Boas."

What, huh, what did he say? I thought.

I felt a hundred eyes, especially those of my new boss, staring at me. I stood there, frozen, to avoid making eye contact with any of the people who were now glaring at me.

The welcome to Atlanta was much nicer than I received in Miami, but I got the feeling that nice welcome was about to evaporate. Six months into my tenure here, and once again, I was stealing someone's job right from under them. This time it was from my boss, Barbara.

I couldn't look at her; I knew she'd be pissed. Hell, I was surprised, even stunned, that she wasn't assigned the job. Of course, I wasn't surprised they chose me; I just never thought they'd choose me over my boss. This was an opportunity for great exposure and advancement, so I was not going hand it off to anyone. *She'll just have to get over it*, I said to myself. *This is my time!*

As the announcements continued, all eyes remained on me. I wasn't sure what they expected. All I could do was stare straight ahead at the line of managers and imagine that soon I would be up there with them. Just the thought of it brought a grin to my face I'm sure everyone noticed. *Who the hell cares?* I thought. *I have arrived!*

The next day, I separated myself from everyone other than the management team, to whom I was now a direct report on this critical and influential project.

Over the next few weeks, I heard the gossip in the hallways, complaints and bitching about the whole thing, especially my role in it. I paid absolutely no attention to it. Even the scuttlebutt down in Miami could be heard in Atlanta. *At least, they wouldn't be bitching about me, I figured. Then, suddenly, I felt ill. They would hate me*, I realized. *I still have a job, a job that will be thrown in their face when I return there, and here they are, about to lose theirs. Shit*, I gasped. *I need them to work with me or I won't get this job done!*

For me to do this job and be successful at it; I would have to return to South Florida, the place I had escaped just six months earlier. The folks who were about to be fired would have to work with me for the next six months.

Less than a week later, I was sitting in a conference room talking with a psychologist assigned to prepare us for confronting the disgruntled employees in Miami.

"What do you mean I may need someone to protect me?" I asked. "Protect me from what? I worked with those people for years!"

I wasn't sure why I was talking to some shrink about needing protection from people I had known for ten years. *Are they crazy?* I thought. I went to the CEO and HR to ask if I could be excused from the therapy sessions.

"It isn't the corporate office employees we're concerned about," the HR representative explained. "The warehouse staff was let go immediately following the announcement and they're already creating security problems at the plant." I rolled my eyes at him. That day, stories from Miami began to circulate.

Threats were being made to both management and corporate employees walking into and out of the building. Tall, wire fences were installed to secure the corporate office and warehouse complex from ex-employees. There was even a security company brought in to man the entrances and exits, roam the warehouse and office hallways, and check people in and out of the property. I decided to sit through the psychological review sessions, just in case.

"Bernadette, you need to influence the staff down there to stay on and work with you and your team to get this system merger done. That won't be easy. Many of them may be really angry," the psychologist said.

"I'm not worried about that. They'll stay if I ask them to. They need the job," I replied. Silently, I wasn't so sure. *Damn, I really need them,* I thought. *I won't get this project done without them. But if they aren't going to cooperate, I'll be more than happy to show them the door. I have a deadline to meet and I'm not going to let them prevent that from happening.*

When I arrived in Miami, I was completely caught off guard when I actually saw the property fenced in behind six-foot wire fences and gates. Suddenly, I felt afraid. When I arrived at the entrance gate, the security guard asked me for identification and my reason for visiting the building.

"Didn't anyone tell you I was coming?" I snapped, trying to appear fearless. "I'm from Atlanta. I'm heading up the system conversion with Joanne. She's expecting me. Lift the gate!" I demanded. The look on the guard's face said everything.

Why the hell am I explaining myself to the security guard? I thought. After a few seconds, he made a call from his walkie-talkie to another guard, who escorted me into the building.

Getting through security turned out to be the easy part; facing the staff I'd worked with for ten years was torture. "Traitor," they said, as I walked down the hallway.

"You knew this was going to happen and saved yourself," they hissed.

What? I thought. Every time someone said something, I was stunned. They didn't hesitate to get right into my face and express their anger at me. I remembered what the psychologist had said: *don't say a thing back to them. Just listen, and then walk away.* That was hard, if not impossible, for me.

After several days, I had finally had enough of their crap. *If they aren't happy about the merger, about me leaving the company, about me coming back to lead this project, too bad! Get over it!* I thought. *This shit has to stop. I have a job to do and they need to support it or get out.* I decided the only way to handle them was to confront them, head on, like I always did.

The next day, I called a company meeting in the second floor conference room, the same room where, just a few short months prior, they had thrown me a going away party, or a 'Go away' party; I wasn't sure which.

As they made their way into the room, you could cut the tension with a knife. The low bickering, crossed arms, and scowls on their faces said it all.

I stood in the front of the room and waited for them to get settled. Then, with a steady, firm voice I said, "We need to address the elephant in the room." That single statement opened up a fire storm of angry comments directed right at me.

Did you know this was happening?

How come they saved you and not the rest of us?

You were always a brown-noser!

What's going to happen to us?

Are you going to be the one to fire us?

We aren't going to work for you just so you can fire us.

I was flabbergasted that they had actually spent time creating a conspiracy theory about my departure. I took a deep breath and gave it to them straight.

"Understand something!" I snapped. "For reasons I am not going to explain to you, I asked for a transfer to Atlanta over a year ago. I wanted out of South Florida, and Atlanta offered me that. I'm sorry to blow your conspiracy theory, but my move had nothing to do with you. It was all about me."

I continued, "Look, whether you like it or not, even if you don't believe me, you have a choice; you can work with me and continue to get paid for it, or you can leave now! It's that simple." Scanning the room, I could see who didn't care about what I was saying, and who was listening, hoping for some great revelation.

I could also see that their armor was slowly being removed and their guards were coming down. *I've got them*, I thought.

"I won't lie," I said. "I can't do this conversion without you. But, don't get me wrong. If all you are going to do is bitch, complain, and lash out at me, you'll be gone with no discussion. No one will stay if they intend to make this hard job even harder. Like I said, you have a choice—stay or leave now! Which is it?"

A few people got up and stormed out of the room, others continued to bicker amongst themselves, but no one left the company.

"Okay then. We have work to do." *The hard part was now over and it was time to get to work.* Or, was it?

Each morning, driving up to the security gate at the employee's entrance, I had to deal with the security guards, showing my ID and verifying why I was there.

"God damn it! You know I am here until this company is shut down, why the hell do you need to card me each and every morning!" I barked at the guard. I didn't care if it was their job to verify all employees. They should have known who I was and saved me the daily delay.

I had never met the head of the security team, but now I wanted to so I could give him a piece of my mind. I never imagined it would send me running for cover and take me off of my game.

Joanne, Miami's newest CEO, had called a last-minute management meeting in her office. As usual, I arrived early. There were three chairs that circled the room. I grabbed the one whose back faced the door and gave me the broadest view. Years earlier, my father had told me, *"If you want to be a central part of every conversation and event going on around you, place yourself in the middle of any given table or room, where you have the best view. The better and wider the view you have, the better the chance you will not miss anything."* It became another part of my FMOAE neurosis. No matter where I am or what type of room arrangement there is, you will find me in the center of it.

A tall man interrupted the meeting to ask Joanne a question. I could see from the corner of my eye that he wore a security guard uniform, but I didn't bother to turn around until I heard his voice.

"Joanne," I didn't hear another word. My heart sank and my body started to tremble. I knew that voice. I shifted to glance at the man behind me. *Holy shit*, I thought. I turned back around to face Joanne's desk. Chills raced up and down my body. The hair on my arms and legs stood on end.

The head of security, the man who would be taking care of everyone, including me, was the same man, who had come to my rescue and then close to raping me a year earlier. Granted, he was drunk and I did manage to get out of there, but I never forgot that night and the terrible fear I felt. Now, months later, he was standing over me in a security guard's uniform. *He's no longer a cop*, I thought to myself. *I wonder if he was fired for sexual harassment.*

I felt like I was going to throw up. I got up, raced to the bathroom, and splashed cold water on my face to calm down before returning to the meeting.

Maybe he doesn't recognize me, I hoped. More than a year had passed and I was no longer a bleached blonde. My hair was cut off above my shoulders and back to its natural red. I was also in a suit, stockings, and heels, as opposed to my Capri's and sandals. Maybe he wouldn't recognize me. A few minutes later, I returned to Joanne's office.

"Are you all right, Bernadette? You turned pure white there for a minute," she said.

"Sure. I must have eaten something bad," I replied.

There was no way I was about to tell her about Zac. I probably should have, just as I should have told someone in authority about that night. It could have gone really bad for me or for someone else in the future. Unfortunately, my getting out of there and putting it behind me was more important at the time.

A few weeks later, I was leaving the building through the front lobby. The voice that came from behind the front desk stopped me in my tracks. "Hey there," he said. "I don't know if you recognize me or not?"

Hesitating, I turned around to find Zac standing in front of me. Trying to appear in a rush, I calmly said, "I do."

"It's good to see you again," he said.

"Thanks," I said, and turned to push open the door and raced to my car.

I loved challenges. I thrived on adversity and pressure, even stress. But God was dishing it out to me in spades these days. *Damn it,* I thought to myself. *I don't need any more stress. I don't deserve this shit! It was bad enough I had to come back to Miami to deal with Ben, and be confronted by angry employees, but to face Zac on a daily basis? That was just plain cruel.* Over the next few weeks, the stress took its toll and the hair at the crown of my head began to fall out.

"What the hell!" I yelled at my reflection in the mirror. I had noticed big chunks of hair on the floor of my shower, but I never imagined I would have a bald spot at the front of my hairline. "Shit!" I screamed.

For weeks, I actually used the 'comb over' technique to cover the nearly inch-long patch of bald scalp at the crown of my head. I was devastated. Sure, years of bleaching my hair with peroxide didn't help, but this baldness had nothing to do with that. I had begun to internalize all the crap happening to me and it was showing up in my body. Well, I was about to fight back; I headed for the drugstore to buy a bottle of Rogaine.

As I stood in the aisle of the drugstore staring at the boxes of balding treatments, I felt nauseous. *How did this happen?* I thought. *Why have I let work shit affect me? Hell, I'm leading this project. I am Superwoman. I should be controlling them, not the other way around.*

And then, like flipping a switch, a new focus and determination burned inside me. I became obsessed with the job I was charged to do, a job I signed up for, a job I knew would bring me the things I passionately wanted. I was not about to allow anyone or anything stop me.

My bitch would make sure of that!

Chapter 16

MORE WITH HONEY
THAN WITH VINEGAR

Debbie sat at The Cove restaurant sipping her white zinfandel, enjoying the stillness of the Intracoastal Waterway and the beat of the Jamaican music floating in from the deck behind us. I wasn't as calm or patient as she was. I had made a long, stressful drive to meet her and it had been a really long week at work.

I had been sitting longer than five minutes, yet the server had not stopped by the table to offer me a drink. In fact, all the young waiters and waitresses were gabbing it up at the cash register, ignoring their tables. I clapped my hands twice to get their attention.

"What are you doing?" Debbie asked, embarrassed.

"It's better than snapping my fingers!" I said. "I'm thirsty and they're just standing over there shooting the shit!"

Looking up from his conversation, the young waiter made his way to our table. He looked annoyed. As he got closer, I could tell that he was not looking forward to approaching us, unsure of what might happen. Before he could hand us the menus, he was distracted by the giggles of a group of young women who walked up to the bar. He stopped dead in his tracks, turned away from us to glance over at the bar, and stood there, watching as his buddies hit on the girls.

"Aghhh!" he sighed, dropping his head back and rolling his eyes. Finally, he turned toward us, approached the table, and threw the menus on the table.

"Are we imposing on you?" I barked. Shocked, he stood there, silent. "If you would rather go and pick up those girls instead of take our order and make your tip, please, go right ahead. Don't let our wallets stop you," I said.

Instead of apologizing, he copped an attitude, asked what we wanted, grabbed the menus, and walked away.

"Wait just a minute!" I yelled. "Why don't you get one of the other servers to help us since you've already lost your tip? They just might want it!"

Now, really pissed, he abruptly turned and went back to the bar to talk with his friends. God only knows what he told them as he pointed over at us.

"You are such a bitch!" Debbie said.

"Excuse me?" I replied.

"Do you really think that was necessary?" she asked. "You better hope he doesn't spit in our food."

"You're kidding me, right? That kid was completely out of line. We are paying customers, plus I do not need to wait for a waiter to finish picking up some chick before I expect my order to be taken!" I snapped back.

"Whatever," she said, as she rolled her eyes and took a sip of her drink. I sat there for a minute, not giving a second thought to the whole incident. Then it hit me. She called me a bitch. *A bitch!* I thought.

No one had ever called me a bitch; not the servers who dealt with me returning food that wasn't just right, not the valets who took too long to retrieve my car, not the assistants who could do absolutely nothing right in my eyes. Heck, not even the boyfriends who dealt with my better-than-thou attitude.

No one had ever even hinted at calling me a bitch. The closest anyone ever came to saying anything close to it was a manager who said, "Bernadette, you get more with honey than you do with vinegar." Rolling my eyes, I'd walked away thinking, *Yeah, yeah, I've heard that before. Tell that to the woman who had to fight every step of the way to the boardroom. She didn't get there by being sweet.*

The way I saw it, a woman had to be strong, aggressive, and act as if she had balls in order to get what she wanted. She was not going to break the glass ceiling by being sweet as honey or a wall flower. And men even seemed to advocate that women be hard-asses. I remembered attending a conference where a male speaker said in front of a crowd of about five-hundred men and women, *"Women, you have to man up if you are going to succeed."* That same attitude permeates not just Corporate America, but American society, as well.

It seems that the term, 'bitch' is a badge of honor. The nastier you are the more press you get, the more readers follow you, and the more people tune in to see what you will do next. The media loves bitches. Even big business thrives on the excitement and audacity of bitches. Think Martha Stewart, Donald Trump, and Simon Cowell, though you would never hear anyone calling Donald or Simon a bitch.

While Corporate America might not champion bitches, it doesn't do anything to prevent them. Corporations fall way short of calling out men or women for obnoxious behavior or coaching them to utilize their skills and talents instead. Rarely do corporate managers confront bitches or alert them to the damage they're doing to their reputation or career; rather, they avoid them.

In many cases where women fail to break the glass ceiling, it's due to their negative, bitchy attitude, not their lack of intelligence or innovation. I began to wish someone had called me a bitch sooner. I've had literally hundreds of performance reviews or appraisals, and not once did anyone ever say to me, *"Bernadette, you are jeopardizing your ability to achieve your goals."* If they had, that might have straightened me out or maybe not.

I know now that I could have achieved my goals by using my skills, talent, and abilities. What I saw during my career in Corporate America indicated otherwise.

I finally learned that lesson while I was still at my job in Miami.

It was the Monday after Black Friday of Thanksgiving weekend. I was called to the CEO's office, never a good thing following a weekend, let alone a holiday sale.

When I reached his office, I noticed Nancy, my boss, standing outside. The CEO's voice boomed through the closed door. I don't know who he was talking to, but things weren't going well for them. I could tell from his voice that he was not happy. Nancy didn't seem concerned. I wondered if that was because my ass was on the line.

I respected Nancy for a lot of things, including her ability to adapt to all of the volatile personalities of the women buyers who worked for her. Watching her handle each of us during a meeting was inspiring. She could stroke Anne, who needed constant affirmation of her work, one minute and be direct and unforgiving to Gina, who didn't like being coddled by anyone, the next. With me, she was straight and direct, never beating around the bush. But when it came to her own ambitions, she was certainly a bitch. You didn't get in the way of her career and when you did, as I did when I left buying to start up a new division, she never let you forget it.

As we stood in the hallway, I knew that if I was about to be chewed out, she wouldn't jump in to protect me, as that could jeopardize her own goals. Once again, I was on my own.

The conference room door opened and Larry and Frank came out, both looking beat up and worn down from their ten-minute encounter with the CEO. Without hesitation, Nancy and I entered the room, shut the door, and sat down at the table across from both the CEO and Satan himself, Ben.

Ben and I had just gotten into a tug of war the week before, so he was looking forward to me getting raked over the coals, and who better to do it than the CEO? Feeling unusually calm, I sat next to Nancy and made small talk. Nancy smirked while Ben sat at an angle looking over at the CEO, waiting for him to pounce on me. I pictured Ben on the sidelines of a boxing match cheering the CEO on, egging him to hit me harder.

The CEO looked up from his papers and said, "Bernadette, what is this? You had inventories three times more than what was budgeted for on the floor going into this weekend's sale. What possessed you to decide on your own to over buy a trendy item by thousands of units for this event?"

"It was easy," I explained. "We blew out of the first shipment at full price, so I merely adjusted for trend, which by the way, called for double the inventory."

Only too willing to throw me under the bus, Ben said, "I told her not to, but as usual, she wouldn't listen and did her own thing."

I didn't even flinch.

"Did you consider the markdowns you were going to have to take to move that kind of volume?" the CEO asked.

"If you look at the profit we generated—not the markdowns, we blew the margins out, as well. I bought that item for fifty cents and sold them, after the markdown, for $1.50. Huge profit! We could have sold them for a $1.00 and still made money. And, we could have sold another fifty-thousand pieces," I stated, confidently.

I looked squarely at Ben and asked, sarcastically, "Wouldn't you agree, Ben, that this was a smart buy?" He didn't say a word; his face said it all. He was pissed.

"Looks that way," the CEO agreed.

Nancy, not one to miss a chance to kiss ass, jumped in and took credit for something she had no part in. "I'm glad you are happy with our decision," she said.

What? I screamed silently. There was no way in hell she was taking any credit for this.

With a voice of mock regret, I said, "And Nancy, I know I didn't involve you on this decision, but I will be sure to do so going forward." Her pale, freckled complexion turned bright red, as she squirmed in her seat.

I glanced over at the CEO and saw a small, devilish smirk on his face. Since the day we raced down I-95 and I flipped him the bird, he knew I didn't take shit from anyone. He shook his head and said, "Good job! We're done here."

Ben looked ready to fall out of his chair. Feeling proud and cocky, I jumped out of my chair and turned to leave.

"Wait!" the CEO exclaimed. "Bernadette, how nerve-racking was this, being it was your first grilling? Were you trembling?"

I approached the table and held my arms out in front of all three of them so they could see the calm in my hands. "Not a bit," I said confidently, looking right at Ben.

If Ben or Nancy thought I would be shaken from that discussion or any like it, they were sadly disappointed. Whether I was the one inflicting my bitch on someone, or someone wanted to make me sweat, I never let them rattle me. What always stunned me was how much people enjoyed watching someone get torn down. Heck, even I enjoyed it.

It would be many years before I would consider shedding any inkling of being cruel, curt, or nasty with everyone. Even if someone, other than Debbie, had told me how much of a bitch I was, I'm confident I would not have listened or believed them There was no way I was ready to hear, believe, and accept that kind of feedback. After all, I was Superwoman!

Chapter 17

LOGIC NEVER SUCCEEDS

I stood in the hallway outside a conference room facing a line of cubicles filled with IT and technical consultants busy at work. An argument was about to break out and everyone would hear it. They wouldn't have a choice. My voice is naturally loud, and well, Steve was pissed.

"You are not invited to this meeting Steve, period. End of story!" I yelled.

"They're my account, Bernadette. I will do whatever I want to do!" he snapped back.

"Not if you want this deal, you won't," I threatened. "I am not going to have a sales guy in there kissing their ass and pushing a sale down their throat when they aren't even convinced yet that they need it." I was there to convince the client that our product would positively impact their business, not guilt them into buying it or discount it for them. "We can do it my way, or not at all. You decide!" I said, turning and walking away.

A year or so before, once again I was pursued and recruited by another company, this time, one of the world's leading database providers. From the day I arrived, I wasted no time making a name, dare I say, a reputation for myself that would continue to feed both my ego and my greed.

Finally, after all my years of retail experience, projects, and success, someone was acknowledging my expertise. I would now leverage that expertise to educate and empower top retail organizations around the world on how to manage and run their businesses more effectively.

The magnitude of the opportunity blew my mind. I ran around in circles in my living room, thinking, *I will be victorious, I will succeed.* I didn't know who I'd be working with but I knew I would be successful. I had no doubt of that. Nor did I doubt that the opportunity would cause my ego to swell to the point of exploding. I made certain everyone in my group knew it, too, including Steve.

The account that Steve was so desperate to close was one of the largest retailers in the country. They were located in South Florida, not far from Boca or Miami. Feeling as if God had it in for me, I was right back in the same damn place I had been running from for years. It was as if South Florida was Alcatraz and there was no escape.

I remember pleading with God, *Why? I go to church. I'm a good person. Okay, sure, I might make it hard for You to forgive some of my sins. But really, must You continue torturing me?*

I imagined Him high in the clouds, sitting on His golden thrown, dressed in white, dark hair blowing in the wind, laughing hysterically every time a plane carried me there. While He was laughing, I was lashing out at anyone and everyone who came between me and the successful closure of yet another project that stood between me and my real home, Atlanta.

When I learned of the assignment with Steve, I went to my new boss, Donald, and begged him to have someone else handle the account. I understood the importance of the account to the company, and even to me, but I was willing to sacrifice the glory on this one. "That is how badly I want out," I pleaded with him.

From the day I met him during the recruiting process, Donald knew that position, power, and money motivated me. We connected so well that I was able to confide in him why I wanted out. But business was business, and Donald was all business. So was I and he knew it. He read me like a book, knowing exactly what buttons to push to get me to do whatever he needed.

"Bernadette, if you help Steve get this account, it will show everyone, including me, the leader you are and the capabilities you have to grow here," he said. He didn't need to say anything more. I accepted the delay on my escape and would help Steve secure the deal.

"Besides", he said, "it's only a two week assignment! You just need to work with their business and technology team, identify the issues they're having, and propose our applications to solve their problems. Easy."

"Easy," I replied. *I can handle two weeks*, I reasoned. I can even avoid having to run into anyone I had run away from. Shortly after that discussion, I was on a plane heading back to Fort Lauderdale. This time however, the skyline was beautiful, the airport was easy to get through, and the people were tolerable. My heart was in Atlanta now; Fort Lauderdale was only a layover.

Being a national sales guy, Steve was very protective of his clients, and more important, his commissions. Those hefty paychecks meant not only food on the table, but also a nice boat, private schooling, family vacations, and a Boca lifestyle. He wasn't going to let anyone derail that.

Frustrated by my lack of cooperation, Steve stormed off to escalate the issue. His real hope was not only to get into the meeting, but to have me removed from his account completely. Knowing that and knowing Donald, I urged Steve to call and talk to Donald directly. That caught him off guard.

As confident as I was in my abilities, Donald was more so. So were other major players in the company, including our new Chairman, who learned in my initiation training a year earlier, that I would be someone to reckon with.

Within a week of coming on board, I was sent to new employee orientation. Along with thirty or so other folks, I sat through five days of boring technical training. Naturally, I challenged the instructors about why I was there. I had no idea what SQL was, what a terabyte was, or what it took to save and store data. I figured tiny elves did it behind my computer screen. And yet, I was hired into the company as a technology consultant.

"It is the only way to get you in", the hiring manager explained. "We don't have roles for your business skill set." *Okay*, I thought, never imagining I would have to do anything technical. *If so*, I told myself, *this would be the first time, ever, that I failed at something*. Nevertheless, I sat through the training and a bunch of boring sessions about bits and bytes, terabytes and kilobytes.

The gentleman at the front of the room was dressed to the nines in a navy suit and tie and starched, white shirt. He rambled on about how to go out to our customers and sell them on how our mega-size database systems would make them successful. After his ninety-minute diatribe, he stopped, turned to the room of almost all men, and said, "Okay, so is everyone good with how to position our solutions to our customers?" Before he even finished his sentence, I raised my hand.

"Yes, do you understand or do you have additional questions?" he asked.

"Neither," I said. "Not only do I not understand, I have enough trouble turning on my laptop and having it run properly. I wouldn't ever go to a customer and attempt to sell them anything on bits and bytes. That is not the way you influence someone that they need what you have to offer," I said. I waited for his response.

"Is that right?" he asked. "If that's so, why don't you come up and explain to us how we should be selling, because as long as I have been here, about twenty-five years, it's what has worked so far," he said.

Jumping up from my chair, happy to talk about anything other than I's and O's, I wiped off a good part of his scribbling from the whiteboard and dove into my explanation. "I know nothing about bits and bytes. I don't care about nor do I want to know anything about them. I am a business user, the one you're developing solutions for. You aren't developing them for the IT guys. So, you need to sell me as to why your solution will benefit and work for me," I said.

The suit abruptly cut me off and said, "When you say 'you', you mean 'we', right?"

I rolled my eyes and nodded. "If we start using technical terms that they don't understand, we might as well pack our bags and leave. We need to sell them on how the business user will benefit from the solution. How it will make their job easier. How it will solve business problems and make the company more money," I added. I scribbled a few points on the board, placed the marker on the table, and went back to my seat.

"You're absolutely right!" the instructor exclaimed. He never even asked me my name. The session ended and I left, feeling proud that in only a couple of weeks, I was able to display my wisdom and knowledge to the company.

A few days later, while leaving the cafeteria after lunch, I blew past the guy in the suit. "Hold up!" he yelled. I turned around toward him. He approached me with his hand extended toward me. "I'm Max. I thought we should meet, as I expect I'll be hearing a lot from you in the years to come," he said. I laughed, introduced myself, and walked away. Once again, I felt confident and cocky. He wanted to meet me, though I had no idea who he was, nor did I care. Only after he became our Chairman did I know who he was.

Now, here I was back in South Florida, dealing with a control freak of a salesman who had it in for me. I waited for Steve to finish his talk with Donald so I could get back to work. I knew Donald. He wasn't pulling me from the account, and he wasn't going to agree that Steve should be in the meeting.

Donald had been with the company for close to thirty years and was recently appointed Vice President of the Retail Division. He was just as ambitious as I was, actually more so. He sought out every opportunity to prove himself to management, and at the same time he was determined to improve the organization as a whole. That determination had him seeking out special projects for himself and his division, and I was right there to support him. The way he saw it, my success was his success, and that bond was evident from the onset.

Since my first job in the gift wrapping department at Weinberg's when I was fourteen, I considered myself an entrepreneur of sorts. I always searched out new innovations, ideas, and opportunities to sink my teeth into. All the while, if those projects helped to advance my career, even better.

Donald was no different. We both knew every new project came with risk, with a challenge. If we did it right and solved the big problem, we would be successful. My willingness to take on those challenging projects, along with the risks, could be very rewarding for him, as well. It made for a great partnership and one we both respected.

Donald was in his mid-fifties and a family man who divided his time equally. They were involved in his business, whether it was traveling with him around the world, or having his ten year old son sit in on conference calls. By the time that kid was fourteen, he could tell our sales team how to sell their accounts. It was impressive.

All the while, he was a power horse when it came to work. He never stopped. With his phone glued to his ear, pager clipped to his waist, and laptop powered on twenty-four hours a day, Donald deserved every promotion he earned. And the moment he mastered one, he was planning for his next.

His forward-thinking and strategic vision made me admire, respect, and in many ways, revere Donald. Like me, he was always three moves ahead. He put his neck out for every new project and tackled it head-on. I loved his attitude and was determined that he use me whenever possible to exploit those opportunities.

The first indication of his risk-taking was when he recognized the need for business expertise, even before the guy in the suit did. Donald began to form a business consulting team of experts to sell our products. Just as I scribbled on that whiteboard about selling from a business user's point of view, Donald's new team was chartered to do the same. A few weeks after orientation training, Donald pulled me out of the technical team and assigned me to his newly-formed business consulting group.

In time, I realized Donald and I had another similar business and success philosophy: you have to spend money to make money.

Since my first buying job in my early twenties, a green piece of felt cloth has hung on the wall behind my desk. Inscribed with yellow writing, it reads, *"You have to spend money to make money."* I proved it with the hundred-thousand, high-margin panties I purchased and many of the other high-volume risks I had taken.

That philosophy, along with our intrapreneurial mindsets, cemented a partnership that allowed me to thrive within the company, in good times and bad. This deal with Steve was one of those high-risk/high-yield opportunities. I would see to that!

Within minutes, the scuttlebutt had ricocheted from South Florida to Atlanta and back to me in the conference room. Donald had simply said, "Steve, you have to trust me. You want her on your team. You may not like how she goes about doing it, but she will get the job done for you. Believe me."

A few minutes later, Steve threw open the door to the conference room. "Fine, have your meeting," he said, "But if you lose this for me…" With that, he slammed the door behind him. That was all I needed to hear. I gathered my laptop and my presentation materials and headed to the boardroom to finish preparing. The meeting would consist of the customer's CEO, leadership team, business team, and me. I had to be prepared if I was going to shine, and I was determined to shine!

When it was over, Steve got the deal, a better deal than even he had expected. He even thanked me, but made a point to emphasize, "You pull that shit with me again and I will throw you off this account."

I laughed loudly and said, "No, you won't!" He rolled his eyes and walked away.

When my two-week assignment was done, despite having won that deal and receiving praise and accolades for it, I flew home to Atlanta pissed and out for blood. I had busted my ass for Steve, Donald, and the company to get the deal. I had even chased two 'Big Six' consulting companies off the account and walked away with nothing but a half-assed 'thank you' that came with a threat. Steve, on the other hand, who never wanted me on the account, walked away with thousands, maybe tens of thousands, of dollars.

I headed straight to Donald's office to raise hell. I planned to argue that Steve had nothing to do with the win. I did everything and deserved that commission more than he did. Sure, as the sales guy, Steve could romance clients with lunch and nice dinners at fancy restaurants and take them golfing. I was doing the heavy lifting and showing them how I could save them millions of dollars. I had earned more than a thank you.

Standing at Donald's his desk with my arms crossed and a scowl on my face, I demanded, "I want a piece of the commission or I don't get another deal for anyone."

Leaning back in his chair, calmly, with his arms folded behind his head, Donald said, "You're being too logical, Bernadette."

"What the hell does that mean?" I blurted. It would be the first of many times over the coming years that Donald would say this.

"It's easy," he continued. "You can be a salesperson and get the commissions if that is what you want."

He knew it wasn't. I was the best at what I did, showing customers how to solve their business problems and saving them millions in the process. I didn't want to be a sleazy salesman. That is how I thought of them. It's why for years I brushed off suggestions by other consultants, sales leaders, and management team members to pursue a sales position. "You'd be great at it, Bernadette," they would say, "and it would double, even triple, what you are currently making." As much as I liked that idea, I wasn't willing to sell my soul.

Donald continued to explain how logical I was being. "Or you can do what you were hired to do and earn your high-paying consulting salary. It's up to you," he said, rocking back and forth in his swivel desk chair, with his usual smirk across his face.

My red, angry face turned even redder and my pulse raced. *Damn it,* I thought. *He knew exactly what to say to get me to back down.* It was *his* logical way of handling me. As the years went by, it wouldn't always be so easy for him.

To me, it was perfectly logical for me to be rewarded for the successes I achieved. Whether that meant money, awards, praise, or promotion, it didn't matter, but it should be something. Being stubborn, I continued to rant, *If you earn something and get results, you get to call the shots—period, end of story.* If that logic didn't work for anyone, so be it. It worked for me and I expected everyone else to line up with it.

Months later, Donald and the account team succumbed to the pressure and gave me the bonus I felt I deserved, the bonus I had earned. While I was grateful for the cash, the vindication felt even better—logical or not.

After all, *it was all about me*, as I told myself through the years. It was that attitude my friends referenced when they gave me their award, my photo in a picture frame with a caption that read, "It's all about me."

It was all about me, until a few weeks later, when Murphy's Law came crashing down on me once again. Any ounce of logic, sanity, and reasonableness went right out the window. Our customer in South Florida called Donald and requested that I lead the twelve-month project I had just sold them. Although I was a fly-in, fly-out consultant, and not an on the ground project manager, Donald agreed.

"What the hell?" I protested. Other consultants would have been overjoyed by the news, but all I heard was the clang of cell doors closing in my Alcatraz of South Florida, the prison I had been trying to escape for years.

I pleaded with Donald but the multimillion dollar deal came with one major stipulation: the client had demanded that I lead the project, or there was no deal. *Shit,* I thought. *This cannot be happening to me again. What the hell?*

I felt as if God was punishing me for the nastiness I was dispensing. I could hear Him chanting in His low, deep voice, *Whatever you do unto others, you do unto me. Damn those Scriptures, stop punishing me,* my thoughts screamed. *I just want out of this town. Please,* I pleaded to the Man above. *Just let me go home. Hell, I'd prefer going back to the grind of traveling to three cities a week. There are other companies that could use my wisdom and expertise,* I vented. *Why are You doing this to me?*

I could have answered that question myself.

Yes, I had maneuvered to kick one person off a project to have someone on the team. I could manipulate more easily. And yes, there were outbursts of underserved anger directed at my team members who worked their asses off, but were never able to please me. And there had definitely been times when

I disrespected managers and bosses, accusing them of not knowing how to do their jobs. I truly believed no one else could ever measure up, be good enough, or be worthy. I never realized it was me who didn't measure up.

Once again, I packed my bags and headed to South Florida.

If I hadn't been a bitch during that first two-week project, I made up for it on my second trip. Like Klinger on the 70's television series, *Mash,* who dressed like a woman hoping to get kicked out of the army, I hoped my inner bitch would get me kicked out of South Florida once and for all. *It wouldn't ruin my career,* I convinced myself; *I'm too good for that.* My skills and talent would trump any attitude I brought to the table. Saying that to myself, over and over again, I began to believe it; besides, no one had ever told me differently.

Chapter 18

MEETING MY NEMESIS

People could fault me for a lot of things, but failing to form strong, talented teams was not one of them. I understood the importance of having smarter, more skilled, and much more talented people on my team, if I wanted to be successful. I remembered a conversation I had with my old boss, Nancy.

"Bernadette, regardless of what you think of these women, they are the best at what they do," she told me. "You don't always get the perfect employee when you go looking for the best. You just need to learn how to maximize their strengths and manage their weaknesses. The effort you make with that will be the difference between your success and your failure."

When it came to my prison sentence of a project, I decided to implement Nancy's advice and pull together the best people in our organization to form the ultimate team. It would be the team that would see to it that the job got done, and got done well. More important, they would ensure I returned to Atlanta for good.

A week later, against the advice of the current team members and my new buddy, Steve, I proposed to bring on another whippersnapper of a talent who I knew would bring fireworks to the team. At the same time, I was convinced she would contribute greatly to the project's successful conclusion—fast!

Her name was Darlene. She was young, bright as hell, and had a 'will do anything' ambition that reminded me of myself. She was a woman at twenty-four, but her petite five-foot, two-inch stature, tiny waist, squeaky voice, and big, blue eyes made her look like a kid. I even called her, "kid," like my old boss, Nancy, had done to me, knowing it would get a rise out of me. Now, it was Darlene's turn to be tortured. I didn't care if she didn't like her nickname. I was her boss and she would have to deal or so, I thought.

The first time I called Darlene, "kid," she stood on her tippy toes, got right in my face, and said, "That will be the last time you call me kid." Despite the scowl on her face, she looked like a real-life Barbie doll who finally decided Ken had played around on her for the last time. She may have been petite, but she was tenacious, hungry, and out for the same blood I was—position, power, and money.

When Darlene first arrived at our company, she began to earn her own 'bitch' reputation. From day one on her first project, she proved she could outsmart and outwork her colleagues, young or old, pro or inexperienced. I saw a great deal of myself in her, and it was both scary and exciting.

Men in the office were intimidated by her, colleagues felt threatened by her, and managers weren't sure how to manage her. I figured Darlene would prove to be either a blessing for me, the customer, and the project or she would be a curse. I didn't care whichever it was, as long as it put me on a northbound plane.

Steve disapproved of bringing Darlene on board. I ignored his feedback and went to the customer project lead, John, to propose the addition. Before I could finish explaining how I thought she could help the project, he pushed back, stating, "She's too inexperienced. She has never been involved in retail and she doesn't even know our business."

True, Darlene was inexperienced in retail and the account's industry. She was ripe out of college. She was much more book smart than retail smart, but I was convinced that her book smarts and knack for detail would allow her to learn the application quickly, master retail, and learn the business inside and out. Her ambition and hunger would guarantee her contribution to the project.

"John," I conceded, "True, she does not have retail experience and she doesn't know your industry. But she's young and ambitious and able to grasp new concepts and applications like a sponge." I then began my own negotiations, "Look, bring her on at no cost to you. If she doesn't prove herself, you haven't lost anything. But, if she proves herself in ninety days, you pay for her at the going consulting rate. Agreed?" John agreed.

Steve was pissed and said I pulled the wool over John's eyes. "I think he's smarter than that, Steve," I said, chuckling. ""Besides, I was her at that age," knowing that would irritate him.

"Great, there'll be two of you," he said, rolling his eyes and walking away.

I did have a few, small worries where Darlene was concerned. *Would we butt heads and create the war of all wars on this project? Was she coachable and manageable, or would her greed and ambition blind her to anyone's direction? Could she jeopardize the success of this project in any way, and therefore jeopardize my career and my flight home?* I would make sure that didn't happen. My career and my ass were riding on it.

As I expected, Darlene dove right into the work, absorbing information like a sponge. She worked tirelessly to learn the various applications and understand the technical aspects that no other business consultant wanted to learn. I saw the motive behind her actions. Within sixty days, John was willing to pay for her. *Ye-hah*, I thought. *Donald will be thrilled; more kudos for me.* I, on the other hand, was ready to throw her overboard.

Her ego grew as fast as her knowledge. She challenged authority, my authority, purposely and with great forethought. She played the same games and maneuvers I did over the years, going over my head, asking to head up parts of the project I assigned to someone else. She forced herself into aspects of the project that were no business of hers and challenged the senior consultants around her.

On one occasion I pulled her from a meeting to set her straight. "You don't invite yourself to meetings, Darlene," I warned. "I will tell you what meetings you can and cannot attend. You will not decide that, nor will you discuss it with the customer. Do you understand?" I asked.

"Well, if you knew what you were talking about, I wouldn't have to invite myself to these meetings!" she countered.

"Excuse me?" I said.

"You aren't grasping the application, and the team needs help," she rebutted.

"Darlene, get this straight. I am not explaining myself to you about why you are on or off a task. You will follow my orders or you will be off this project. Do you understand?" I asked again, getting more pissed. She never did get it. If she did, she wasn't going to admit it. Every day, I knew I'd be in for a fight from someone ten years younger, three inches shorter, and an easy fifty pounds lighter, with a mouth that all too often stirred up familiar memories.

Reading through notes from her performance appraisals, I saw my scribbles in the margins that read, "audacity," "nerve," "curt," "manipulative," and "ruthless," to describe her. What caught me off guard was these were the same words that had been used to describe me.

On one occasion, I sat her in front of my laptop to show her exactly what she wasn't getting. She sat with her head cocked, arms and legs crossed, and a smug, "I'm better than you" look on her face.

"Let me show you, Darlene, what you don't get!" I said. Irritated by having to do this again, I said, "Unless you are sitting here each and every day that Donald, Steve, Rob, the CIO, and Pat, are reaching out with questions and issues, you, my dear, sweet Darlene, have no clue as to what you are talking about. So, for the last time, I won't have you questioning me or my decisions. Do your job and all will be good. Understand?" Like a Ferris wheel that never stops going around in circles, she said she understood, but continued her relentless badgering. I thought, *God is paying me back, big! He sent an exact copy of me to teach me a lesson—about me!*

Since getting home was more important to me than dealing with a smart-ass girl, I continued to remind myself why I'd hired her. Before long, I realized what she was up to. Like me, she had a three-step plan. She was targeting my job. I couldn't believe I didn't see that the moment she came onto the project. If Darlene thought that she was my competition, she was wrong. She wouldn't be getting my job any time soon. If she did, it would be from my moving on and up—not out.

It was becoming more and more evident that our greed and ambitions were putting everyone on the team and the project itself at risk. Our deafening voices shook the walls of the third floor.

It came to a head one evening, as the team hunkered down for a long night of data modeling, a project that was weeks behind schedule. I was asked to take over. The first challenge was to spend the day with three brilliant technical geeks who were consumed with one-upping the next guy. As much as I respected each of them individually, the idea of being locked in a small conference room with them was unbearable.

Exhausted and mentally wrecked, I returned to my hotel to freshen up and change my clothes. Walking through the lobby, I noticed our managing partner, Rob, sitting at the bar. Needing a drink, I dragged myself up to the bar, dropped my ass onto the stool next to him and ordered a beer.

"So," I said loud enough for the bartender to hear. "What do you get when you put three CTO's in a room for eight hours?"

Rob just looked at me and laughed. "I have no idea."

"A god damn migraine" I yelled.

He laughed and said, "Well, get the model right and you won't have to go through that again." *Yeh, yeh, yeh*, I thought, wanting to smack him for dampening my joke.

I finished my beer and went to the room to change my clothes before heading back to my home away from home. When I arrived, my team was sitting in a small conference room with papers of model diagrams laid out across the table. But none of them had a pencil to paper; they were just sitting and talking. "What are you doing?" I asked the group.

Darlene, the apparent ring leader of the discussion stated, "Well, before you interrupted us, we were discussing what business data we were missing on the model. Maybe you could tell us."

"Excuse me?" I snipped.

"Well, you're obviously questioning whether we're working or not. I figured you could tell us by just looking at the model," she said.

"What are you doing, Darlene?" I asked, growing more pissed. *Don't let her get to you*, I said to myself.

Realizing I wasn't succumbing, she said, "We are trying to find the missing data. We know it's here; we just can't seem to find it. How did you enjoy your nap at the hotel while we were here working?"

"That's it, come with me" I commanded, walking around the table to escort her to the hallway. "Now!" I barked.

I closed the door behind us and we walked away from the room.

"Where the hell do you get off, Darlene?" I raged, feeling my face grow redder and redder. "One last time, I won't have you or anyone else talk to me like that." Remembering her motives, "Understand Darlene, if and when I leave here, you will not be the one to replace me. I know you think you will sweetie, but kiddo, you won't! You know why? Because, Donald, Rob, and more important, the customer CIO will look to me to recommend who can lead this group to the successful completion of the project. And don't be fooled thinking you are loved by them or any of the people in that room," I yelled, pointing to the closed conference room door. I chuckled. "They aren't blind to what's going on down here."

Her cocky mug went blank. She stood there, staring over at the conference room door, where we both knew the team had a glass up against the wall, listening to our fight. I walked over and threw open the door and shouted, "Okay, let's get to work!"

Darlene had never considered that I, too, had the ear of the customer. I wasn't going anywhere, no matter how loud anyone on either team screamed. If I did, the customer CIO would want me to decide who should lead it up. Darlene hadn't counted on that.

Since I'd first arrived on the customer account for the initial, two-week project, the CIO and I hit it off. It wasn't for my pleasing demeanor as much as it was for my laser focus and tenacity for delivering results to his company. Within those two weeks, I ousted two of the 'Big Six' consulting companies he wanted to bid for the job. On another occasion, having shown him how loyal I was to my customers, he asked me to sit in on competing vendor presentations to offer him and the leadership team my objective opinion. The vendors were floored.

The CIO knew that I favored no one. I spared no one. If something went right, the individual or the team received congratulations. When something went wrong, was delayed, or didn't happen, everyone heard it—his team, my team, our management, and his management.

One morning, he approached me and said, "We're moving your team and their offices down to the basement."

"The basement?" I asked, shocked.

"Yes, the basement. But you will be staying right here," he said.

"What, right here? Where? I won't be with my team? I can't do that. I need to be with them." Frantic, I continued to grill him. "What is this really about?"

The CIO had inquired several times over the last few months about the obvious tensions between my team and me, more specifically, tensions between Darlene and me. "You are being awfully hard on your team, Bernadette. They have been here through the weekends for a month now, working until midnight."

"You're right, they have been. But we have a deadline to meet, and we are going to meet it." I rebutted.

We did have major deadlines, the project was behind, and there was no end in sight unless we made up weeks of time. I was even forced to take up lead on several technical activities, despite my own admitted lack of experience. "You don't need to do the work, just oversee it so it gets done," Rob stressed to me.

I convinced the CIO that the team was fine, that I was fine, and there were no tensions that needed addressing. Now, I needed to convince him not to send us to the basement. "We are starting renovations on the entire third floor this weekend, so we are moving all vendors to the basement," he explained.

"Vendors" was a nice way of saying all of the high-payed, 'Big Six' consultants; Ernst and Young, IBM, and Arthur Anderson, that had offices in the dungeon of the basement. It now included us. I had taken great pride in the fact that since day one, long after those other vendors were on board and placed in the dungeon, my team and I were located on the same floor with the users and the management team. I didn't want to see that change.

"To the dungeon you mean," I said, trying to laugh it off. "Why am I not moving down there with them? It's important for me to be with my team," I said. *Why would he have me running up and down between floors just for that convenience?*

"I like having you outside my office," he responded.

Say what? I thought. I said, "I don't understand."

"With you sitting right outside of my office, I can hear everything you say," he explained. "Whether you're arguing with one of my team members about deadlines or fighting with your own management to get us what we need, you fight to the end. You don't care who it is. If they aren't getting the job done, you're right on them. I like that."

I couldn't help but laugh. "You have got to be kidding!" I chuckled.

"Nope," he said, and that was that.

"I guess that's one advantage of a loud, baritone voice!" I laughed and turned away.

I went to announce the move to the team. Still laughing under my breath, I remembered all the times on the phone with his team arguing over how the account was being handled. *Shit,* I thought. *I never realized that all of the discussions I have ever had in that office could be heard.* Well, maybe I did and didn't care. That was more like it.

It didn't matter to him if I was a bitch about it or not; I got what his project needed. From that day on, I knew where I stood with him and

Darlene soon learned it, as well. She never should have doubted that I was more skilled at this bitch thing than she was.

The team was thrilled about the move. What I heard from behind cubicle walls and through the conference room door cracks, they would now be away from the eyes and ears of the customer, and best of all, me. "At least it will be a lot quieter," I overheard one say. My aim and fire now had to go three stories down for my bitch to shoot them in the back. Everyone was happy, at least for now.

What started out as my intention to provide a smart, young woman with an opportunity for growth actually did turn out to be my ticket home. The project was finally wrapping up. Exhausted, drained, and burnt out, I returned home to Atlanta.

As expected and deserved, over the next several months, the team was showered with awards and recognition, just what Darlene and I craved. At the division's awards dinner that year, the project team members and I walked onto and off of the stage at least six times to receive accolades for the achievements we made in South Florida. Piled in our arms were stuffed animals, American Express gift certificates, and paper award certificates that read, "Customer Account of the Year," "Project Team of the Year," and for me, "Consultant of the Year."

As the evening came near its end, the doozie of all awards was announced. This last award was the single, most important award of the year for anyone on the sales and consulting teams. It was the 'you have arrived' award, the *Consulting Excellence Award*. Not only did it mean you went above and beyond for your team and your organization, but it meant you went above and beyond for your customer—which for me was the reason, outside of personal gain, we did what we did. Though I was sitting in the back of the banquet room, I heard the announcement loud and clear: *The winner of this year's Consulting Excellence Award is… Bernadette Boas!*

Surprised, I jumped up and made my way from the back of the room, winding through the tables. I stood tall with my head up, shoulders back, and chest out. *I had arrived.* All the way to the podium, I felt my father walking beside me. He taught me that if you work hard, put everything into it, and deliver great, not good, you can never lose. He knew that losing or failing was not in my vocabulary, let alone in my business acumen.

A week later, the bigger announcement was made. This year's Consulting Excellence award trip was to Dubai, United Arab Emirates. *Dubai*, I thought. *Shit! That is so cool!* I was so excited; I picked up the phone and pager to let everyone know it. Not only would this award give me the chance to see one of the finest, wealthiest places in the world, but it validated that I was the best at what I did. *Yeee-haa!* I cheered to myself. *I have arrived!*

Not everyone was happy about my award or my recognition. Colleagues from the local office as well teams around the country commented, "If I knew that making a project difficult to work on would get me to Dubai, I would have made my project horrific." Or they would say, "Are you proud that you put your team through hell to achieve that award?" The one that really made me laugh was, "Darlene got that award for you!" I couldn't stop laughing at that comment. *Idiots*, I would whisper under my breath.

Despite all the comments, I loved the attention, the praise, the glory, and the taste of victory. I even loved the competition, adversity, and resentment other people showed me. I saw it as their weakness, not mine, and actually relished their animosity. When it came to my team, I wouldn't allow anyone to lash out at them. No matter what happened on the inside of the project, they worked their asses off and deserved those awards. Darlene deserved it, too, if only for her ability to grasp the applications and service the customer. *She'll learn*, I thought. *She has to if she wants to gain the position, power, and money she craves. She's not a dumb girl.* What I learned about myself was regardless of what others thought, my team was still my team. I would fight to get them what they deserve.

I tried to recall the toxic environment in which the project succeeded, but couldn't. Maybe I didn't want to. If I had, I would have explained it away as everyone else's fault, not mine. The glory, praise and adulation were enough to make me forget those dark days and move on to my next conquest, which would continue to feed the ugly bitch and ego that consumed me.

Chapter 19

THE BEGINNING OF THE END

Over the next several years, I experienced more success, as well as more adversity, both at work and at home. Oblivious to the toll the years of stress and strife were having on my body, spirit, and soul, I forged ahead, still determined to make a name for myself, even if that name was BITCH!

Donald, my mentor and biggest supporter, continued to encourage my intrapraneurial spirit. He allowed me to charter unknown waters in search of new ways to improve the productivity and operations of the field organization. In turn, he cheered me on to find new ways to enhance both his position and ultimately, mine. He egged me on to leverage my "tough love" approach, as he saw it, to get teams around the country to deliver their customer projects.

The year before, we had rolled out a new enterprise application and a number of the large customer projects were spiraling out of control. Many customers put the squeeze on Donald and threatened, "Get it done or get out!" So for close to a year, he used me as his one-woman covert operator and dropped me in to accounts to clean up the messes. It didn't hurt that the customers were among the Fortune 100 retailers. I was not going to be the cause of one of our top accounts throwing us out. That risk was the adrenaline I needed to leverage my bitch to the max. I believe Donald thought so, as well. I took full advantage of the visibility and the whip I was given, and made sure the projects, and I, were successful.

That whip came in handy as I began my year-long trek into the wilds of a small town in Arkansas, where you had to step over cow dung to get from the plane to your rental car. Our team was failing miserably to implement a multimillion dollar application for the customer. The customer's CIO made it crystal clear that if we didn't get it implemented, we would be taking it home with us. *Great*, I thought.

"How long do I have?" I asked him, not wanting to hear the answer.

"Thirty days!" he replied.

"You have got to be f*** kidding," I said.

"Nope, so get it done," he said and walked away. The next day I was on my way into the fiery den of one of our largest customers to whip my team— and maybe the customer—into shape.

When I got off of the plane, I headed straight to the motel bar, the only bar in town, to meet the team. When I did, it was like I had stepped back in time and was part of an old cowboy movie. Dressed in a black, lycra pantsuit with big, gold, hoop earrings, red lipstick, and big, red hair, I stuck out like a sore thumb.

As I pushed the door open, the smoke poured out into the hallway and the cloud of fumes was so thick, I had a hard time seeing anything, even the hostess who greeted me at the door.

"How can I help you sweetie?" she asked, with the deepest Southern drawl I had ever heard. She looked like Flo from the 70's sitcom, *Alice*.

I choked back laughter and said, "I'm looking for a group of consultants," she cut me off before I could finish what I was saying.

"Oh sweetie, they're over in the corner by the pool table." I thanked her and went to meet up with the team.

Several of the team members had worked for me already. Not one of them had a smile on their face when they greeted me. They knew that if I had been called in to their project, some heads were gonna roll. I told them we weren't talking business tonight and that we would get started first thing in the morning. I flagged down the waitress to order a round of beer. I never expected her to ask, "You're not from around here are you, sweetie?"

"No siree, Ma'am, I am not," I said, mocking her accent.

"Yeh, I could tell," she said as she turned to get our beers.

"What was that about?" I laughed and asked the group.

"Well, look at you Bernadette. They don't exactly wear black here, or big, gold earrings and rings." I laughed again.

The waitress came back and handed me my beer and our check for a whopping fifteen dollars. "Fifteen dollars? For a dozen beers? Oh, that is precious," I said to the group, laughing even harder.

It was good we had a few laughs that night because the next day, we began a solid month of seven-day work weeks, twelve-hour days, and constant hammering. "If you can't get this done, I will find someone who will!" I threatened, or, "How do you not know how the hell it is supposed to be done? You've been working on it for months!" I screamed.

A few of the team members had been on the project, away from home and living in hotels, for several months. "I'd like to go home for at least one weekend," Rick said.

"You'll have all the weekends you want if you don't get this job done. Now, stop complaining and get back to work," I snarled. The four-week operation was not easy or fun. The customer was ruthless when it came to delays or mishaps. My team caught hell, not from the customer, but from me. I was their front line and although I would protect them from others, no one protected them from me. I had a job to do. They had a job to do. Together we had to make these projects successful. A happy customer meant more promotions, raises, and accolades for me—that's all that mattered.

By the end of that year, I had racked up platinum status on my airline memberships, earned baskets of flowers and candy from my hotel chain, and gained too many pounds from eating pasta and drinking beer. But I was drowning in misery. When I returned home one steamy, hot August day from one of those many trips, it all came crashing down around me.

I wandered the parking lot at the Atlanta airport for thirty minutes, unable to remember where I parked my car a few days earlier. Week after week of flying out on Monday mornings and flying in on Friday afternoons made it hard to remember where I parked my car, what rental car agency I booked with, and even which clothes were clean. Surrounded by hundreds of cars, I paced the deck that I always parked my car on, but it was nowhere. Hot, tired, and frustrated, I broke down in tears. The tears were not for my missing car; I knew it was there somewhere. I needed a new challenge, a new project. I never dreamed that assignment would take me from exhaustion to the brink of a heart attack.

With a couple of other assignments behind me since the Arkansas trip, our Chairman and CEO introduced a new, strategic initiative that would change the way our organization did business. Standing next to him as the announcement was telecasted live around the world, I was beaming—standing up tall, with my shoulders back and my chest out. I couldn't have been more excited, because this latest challenge, of course, had come with all of the trappings: promotion, title, and money.

Donald had advanced to a global consulting position years earlier. He brought me with him to take an industry initiative I had been leading up for him in Retail, to the global field organization. This project would provide tools, processes, and means for our team to work together, regardless of location. It would save and make our customers and our company millions of dollars. And it would be my ticket to senior management. I would be one step closer to leading my own company.

And now our Chairman and CEO was announcing to the world that our field industry initiative was one of the company's top five global strategic initiatives. It was the first time a field initiative went global.

Not everyone was pleased that Donald and I were tasked to head it up. Although we had introduced the concept to the organization when we first implemented it more than two years earlier, one division declared that if they weren't responsible for heading up the project, they wouldn't contribute to it.

Donald never wanted to admit it, but it was obvious to me from day one that the Marketing team was going to make our lives, especially mine, hell. It should have been the first of many red flags that this assignment was going to make any previous covert operation look like child's play.

I diverted any plans they had to derail the initiative and unseat me, when I changed my title from VP to Chief Knowledge Officer, proudly announcing it on that initial broadcast with the CEO. That action so enraged the Marketing division that they and their leader, a member of the senior management executive team, refused to come to the announcement. He remained in his office upstairs. I thought, *The team in Miami had sharp claws, but Dayton would make Miami's claws seem like kittens kneading my back.*

Immediately following the meeting, I set out to bring together the groups within the organization to lay out the plan of attack for delivering this major initiative to the field, Marketing included. Pumped up and ready to rock and roll, I anxiously awaited that first corporate-wide meeting. I expected everyone to be on board. They weren't.

"We cannot and will not dedicate people to this initiative, Bernadette. It's not something we need," said Tina, a member of the Marketing division. Her voice was full of disdain.

"Marketing is a critical division that creates, distributes, and reuses field data, Tina," I implored. "How can you say you don't need this?"

"We just don't," she remarked. For the rest of the meeting, she sat in her chair with her nose turned up to the group.

Son of a bitch, I thought. This wasn't Tina speaking; this was Beth. Tina's boss had been a no-show for every meeting and discussion around this initiative. Again, that should have been a red flag.

After the meeting, I vented my frustrations to Donald. "This is a corporate strategic initiative, Donald. How can they say 'nope, we aren't playing'?"

"You're being too logical again, Bernadette. They just did." he said.

"Okay, then help me. Help us," I pleaded. "We need them on board and I don't need to fight with them the entire time!"

"Just see how it goes," he said. Another huge, red flag waved by, unnoticed. This was not going to be easy and we hadn't even started yet.

All of the other divisional groups were on board. They were thrilled that someone was finally including all of the relevant business teams on a project. In the past, business teams developed a new initiative on their own, not wanting other departments to influence what they were working on. The Marketing division was notorious for this approach.

I forged ahead, ignoring their tantrums.

Despite the wall the Marketing division built around me, over the next couple of months, I worked tirelessly to finalize the company-wide business plan. I made every attempt to engage Beth and her team on the plan and the presentation to the Board. What happened next proved me to be a novice compared to the cunning, back-stabbing, and manipulative acts that Beth and her team executed.

When I returned to the office after the board presentation, I found Donald typing away frantically on his laptop. "You're not going to believe this!" I blurted, as I stormed into his office, not giving a thought to whether he was busy or not.

"What are you talking about, Bernadette?" he asked distracted.

"Beth presented the same damn initiative to the board that I did!" I shouted. "The same exact one!"

"Keep it down. Marty's in his office preparing for a meeting," he warned. Marty was the CEO. "What do you mean, 'the same one'?"

I explained, "I was invited into the conference room where all of the vice presidents were presenting their initiatives to the board. As I walked into the room, I heard Beth's voice over the speakerphone. She didn't know I was there, nor did she expect me to be. The next thing I heard her say was, 'We feel this initiative will provide the Marketing team and then the organization, exactly what we need to create, share, and reuse the data that the field teams are gathering. We would start it small, test it thoroughly and then roll it out, so our costs are low.'"

Donald sat still, squinting with confusion. "She wrapped up. Bruce thanked her. Then I was cued to begin my presentation. Not even ten minutes into our presentation, Bruce says to me, 'Bernadette that sounds like the exact initiative that Beth presented us. Is it'?"

I could tell from the look on Donald's face that I was about to lay down a bomb, a bomb we would be cleaning up for a while. "I told Bruce directly, 'It certainly sounds that way, Bruce. I'm just as confused as you are. We've involved Beth and her team in establishing this business plan based on the corporate strategic initiative Marty assigned to Donald and me, so I'm not sure why she is presenting the same one.'"

Donald stood up as I continued to rant. "Then Beth jumped in and said, 'It isn't the same one Bruce. This plan is specific to the Marketing division and has its own requirements.'" *Unbelievable*, I thought. *What a bitch. Instead of partnering with us, she defined her own strategy and proposal.*

Beth and her boss, Ron, had been at the company for years. From what I could tell so far, they got their positions not for their skills and talents or even for their cunning and manipulative management style, but whose asses they kissed. Ron was raised at the company and Beth rode his coattails. I began to understand why so many people in her division were already exasperated when they first met me. "Now there's two of you? Damn!" they would say.

"But Bruce wasn't having it," I said. "He cut Beth off and said to both of us, 'Ladies, it sounds to me like the exact same proposal, company-wide or divisional. The two of you need to figure out who should present it and be sure there is only one set of numbers budgeted for it. We won't launch two identical initiatives.'"

"I wanted to reach into the phone and strangle the living shit out of her," I said. My heart was racing like a thoroughbred, and my already-high blood pressure was spiking. Donald could see from the fury in my eyes that I could have choked her had she been in the same room.

"Do you believe it?" I asked him, drained. A red flag should have gone up when Donald accused me, once again, of being too logical.

"They're already fighting you every step of the way," he said with frustration. "What makes you think you can ever get them to work with you even if we have only one initiative?"

"Where are you going with this, Donald" I snapped. *He doesn't get it, why doesn't he get it?* I wondered. I was determined to make this project successful. This initiative was so important to me, it had to work.

Donald had been with the company for close to thirty years. I should have read between the lines and heeded the red flags. While I would have preferred to fly solo on this initiative, it had to be different this time. If we succeeded, it would not only transform the business, but Donald's and my careers, as well.

Growing more frustrated than empathetic, Donald finally said, "You two obviously can't work together, Bernadette, this has been going on for months. Why don't we just give it to them to handle?"

"Give it to them? Are you f*** serious?" I asked incredulously. "I've been working on this initiative for years, not weeks like Beth, Donald. You know I have worked my ass off, and now you want me to hand it over?" I couldn't contain the anger welling up and escaping in obscenities from my mouth. He was getting angry, but I wasn't letting it go. It meant too much to me since I had proposed it to him several years back.

"What do you think is the opportunity here, Bernadette?" Donald asked, when I initially suggested the project.

"We have consultants all over the world implementing the same applications and the same processes," I explained. He smirked and paced like a caged animal. "Yet, our teams are not sharing that information with each other. If we could give them the tools to create work products on their own or across projects, and then collaborate to share best practices, everyone would be much more productive and profitable."

"What do you think?" I asked, knowing he would agree. He wanted to know how we'd pull it off. I never worried about the how. I had proven time and again that I would get the job done, whether I started with a blank piece of paper or had teams of experts with all the answers. This initiative would be no different.

It didn't take long for Donald to approve it and assign me to lead the initiative for the Retail division. Thinking three steps ahead, I told him once we were successful in implementing it here, we could roll it out across the globe, together. He agreed. I never dreamed I would rue the day I told him about it.

This latest promotion meant a great deal for me and came with the usual perks. But this time it was different. For the first time in my career, the money, power and authority were not as important as my passion for the project and making a difference to the organization. Unfortunately, no one, including Donald, saw that. He saw me as the tough, demanding, greedy young woman he had met ten years earlier. What neither of us knew was that my greed was diminishing, and his was accelerating to the point that loyalty no longer mattered.

Over the next couple of months, Donald retreated from fighting for our mutual passion. He made it clear that this would be my battle to fight alone. All these years we had strategized together, innovated together, and motivated each other, and now he was abandoning me. I was crushed, disappointed, and ashamed of him and told him so. He sat across the table, as I fought back tears and said to him, "I am so disappointed in you, Donald. I can't believe that with everything we've been through, all I have done for you, you're abandoning me." He never even looked up.

Ron and Beth got what they wanted. Donald had decided that his own position, power, and greed were more important and turned on me. Even if this was about me, the man I revered had never once raised an issue or concern he had with me.

I didn't care what happened to me. I knew the contributions I made, the successes I had, and how much I did for the most important people I served, my customers. That day, Donald proved the old adage, *"the higher up you go, the lonelier it gets."* My Global Vice President office got very quiet that day. And for the first time in my career, I welcomed it.

In the months that followed, my entire life began to shift. My bitch, my insatiable greed and ego, was dying and I was moving toward rediscovering the passion. I had lost my passion for everything—work, social life, and relationships. I was now losing interest in the antics of other bitches, even those of Beth and Ron.

If God is for me, who could be against me?

Chapter 20

THE WALLS COME CRASHING DOWN

"Where the hell do you get off proposing the same initiative you knew I would be presenting?" I yelled at Beth over the phone. Realizing I was on my own and Donald wasn't fighting for the project, I went on the war path. She might be fooling Bruce and the others on the board, but she wasn't fooling me. I wasn't going to let her think I was going to roll over dead, just because she had the audacity to go against the CEO's direction.

"Bernadette, we are perfectly capable of handling this project ourselves. We don't need you and your team to do it for us," she replied condescendingly.

"Beth, you aren't that ignorant to the fact that global initiatives are just that—global, all encompassing. They require all the teams to support each other. Why is it you need to be a cowboy on this?" I asked.

"Because we can do it better than you," she said, matter-of-factly.

Bitch, I thought. Then I said, "What the hell is the issue you have with me and my team, Beth? Are you so threatened or intimidated by me that you can't fathom relinquishing control to me? God forbid I'm successful. Is that it?"

Silence.

Well, well, well, I thought. *I hit a nerve.*

Beth was a control freak. I knew that, but I didn't think she would really let her ego and insecurity block a major initiative from actually happening. But in her mind, she wasn't doing any such thing. After all, if the tables were turned and she owned this strategic initiative, I would have been digging my claws into it. From day one, her bitch of insecurity was gunning for the entire project and for me. She wasn't going to give up until it was hers.

I'm done, I thought, as I slammed down the phone. I didn't know what that meant or where it would lead me, but at that moment, I needed to get away from everything and everyone. The very idea of having to talk to or see her, Ron, or Donald made me ill.

I had no desire to look into Donald's eyes. I couldn't bear to see his betrayal. He finally gave into his greed and ego and was turning on his own people. He didn't even have the courage to confront me, be honest with me, protect, or support me. In an instant, or what seemed like it, I no longer revered, trusted, or respected him. In fact, I was disgusted with all of them— Ron, Beth, and Donald.

Exhausted, drained, and emotionally beaten down, I became a zombie, walking through my days like one of the living dead. Instead of jumping out of the bed each morning when the alarm went off, I buried myself under my blanket, refusing to face another day.

My mind and heart were empty as I trudged through each day. I felt like I was wading through quicksand, continually being pulled under. I spent more time on my couch in my pajamas than I did in the office in a suit. I preferred phone meetings versus face to face. Nearly devoid of any passion or desire for the work, the company, and the people, I worked in solitude. It was the only way to stay sane and avoid unleashing my bitch on all of them. But oh, how I wanted to!

Many days, I sat in my home office, rocking back and forth in my swivel chair, wondering how the hell this all happened. When I couldn't figure it out sober, I tried to work it out in an emotional, drunken stupor. I couldn't believe all my years of working my ass off, giving everything I had, and being as loyal and dedicated as anyone could be had come to this! And no one cared.

The quicksand was winning the fight. I was going under and had no idea how to pull myself up. Over and over again I would ask myself, *Who is this emotional, vulnerable, and angry woman? This isn't me!!*

I was thrilled when February 2007 came around. It was time for the company's annual kick-off meetings, which meant I would travel thousands of miles away from the drama in Atlanta and Dayton. In previous years, the tour of regions went through Berlin, Hanoi, and Prague. Each trip gave me a much-needed vacation and time to recharge and reload my 'bitch.'

This year, I was off to Phuket, Thailand, where tranquility, privacy, and pampering awaited me. For four glorious days, I would submerge myself in sleep, quiet, and food before going to the other side of the island for three days of meetings with the very people I was trying to flee. My plan was to be refreshed and rejuvenated for whatever my changing world would throw at me.

I didn't realize how exhausted I was until I woke up thirteen hours into the fifteen hour flight. Adjusting how I was laying in the first class flat bed, I rolled over onto the tall bottle of water the flight attendant had laid at my side. When she realized I was awake, the attendant raced over, relieved. She said I had been asleep so long, she feared I had died. I couldn't help but laugh out loud. It was the first laugh I had had in many months.

While in Phuket, I felt like a zombie. For hours, I lay on the pristine, white sand beach. There were no books, no music pouring from my Nano, and no conversations with fellow tourists who were sprawled across the sand. It was as if a "no vacancy" sign hung from my mind, heart, and soul. Even when I sat at a gorgeous, oceanside table in a majestic, thatched-roof restaurant, I was unfazed. I simply sat, gazing out onto the moonlit water, staring aimlessly at the glass of wine that sat in front of me.

That was a shift from the months leading up to this trip. Though I didn't drink alone at home, I certainly found comfort in martinis and beers when I didn't want to expose my true self—the insecure, intimidated, undeserving one—to others. *What if they didn't care for the real me?* I wondered. So many nights out with friends or men I cared for, or colleagues who I respected turned into evenings of too much drinking and even fighting. I pushed men and friends away and turned mentors and colleagues into non supporters. No amount of money, power, or position masked the self-afflicted mental and emotional wounds like a Kettle One vodka martini, straight up, dry with a couple of olives. On this night, it was a glass of wine and I had no desire for it. I stared out at the glittering flickers of stars in the Phuket sky.

By the time I made my way over to the other side of Phuket for the company meetings, I was determined to engage, collaborate, relate, and team with my business friends and foes.

When I arrived, I was ecstatic to find that none of my foes would be in attendance. I would be able to enjoy a few days with my Aussie and Asian business pals. One evening before the trip ended, we enjoyed an evening of hysteria at a game rifle shooting range. For one full hour, I took my anger and disappointment out on helpless stuffed animals that Brent, Carl, and I secured to paper targets. By the time I was done, the white stuffing of the big-eyed, red Martian was missing, multiple shots ripped the felt clothing, and the poor guy was missing one ear. I felt great! I also felt vindicated.

When I returned home, I found that trouble continued to brew in the hallways of the Atlanta and Dayton offices, and for once it had nothing to do with the raging feud between Beth, Ron, and me.

Ron, the Executive Vice President, didn't know me from Adam. Like Beth, we had never worked together nor engaged with one another prior to this last assignment. For reasons only he knew, he decided I wasn't good enough to play in his sand box. It didn't matter to him that every project I had ever implemented had been successful. If he and his team weren't leading an initiative, it wasn't worth supporting. Ron didn't want me on the project, and didn't feel I could do the job. During one of my visits to Dayton, he made a point to tell me so.

"Excuse me Ron," I said, stunned that he had confronted me. "Have we ever worked together? Have we ever engaged or even gotten into a tiff together?" He didn't respond. "If we've never worked together and I've never worked with Beth or her team, how do you know what I'm capable or not capable of doing?" I continued, "I would hate to think that a senior leader of this company is listening to gossip rather than engaging and observing someone to make their own assessment. At worst, I would hate that your agenda and motives are blinding you to what's best for the company."

"I just don't think you're the best person for the job," he said flatly.

"That's too bad, Ron, because Marty and Donald think I am, and my record proves it," I said. He turned and walked out.

Sitting back in my chair, staring at the door he had just exited, I felt exhilarated from the release of my pent-up anger. Yet the minute I said those things, I knew my fate was sealed. Ron was the stereotypical corporate white shirt who had his pets and those he ignored. I knew my days were numbered. When I told Donald, he said, "No, you're fine." But his eyes told a different story. They darted from left to right, never once landing on me. It was apparent that I wasn't fine. *Damn him,* I thought, *why couldn't he just say that?*

From that first company-wide meeting, when Marty announced the global initiative and Ron stayed behind in his office, it was hard for me to have respect for him. It was harder to overlook the fact that he was also the next in line to replace Marty as CEO. That was something Donald probably didn't want to think about, since becoming CEO was part of his three-step plan. For years, the two of them constantly jockeyed for their positions. This time I may be the victim of their political games. I just didn't care anymore.

The days of my wanting to work my ass off for Donald, to provide ideas and strategies to grow our division, and give my unwavering loyalty, were gone. I couldn't work with or for people I didn't respect and at that moment, I didn't respect any of them.

The rumble through the halls was getting louder. Everyone from the CEO to the division's leadership teams, including Donald's, was feeling it.

A major shift was in the works, not just for the company, but for me, as well. I just wasn't sure what it was. I did know that over the last several months, as I fought off the claws of those who wanted me to fail, I was losing my maniacal need to control. My desperate need to know everything and to be in the inner circle was dissipating. My FMOAE was diminishing and quite frankly, I was growing disgusted watching people lash out at and tear people down.

Over the last eight or nine months, people I had once admired and respected turned ugly and selfish. Here I had been the ultimate corporate bitch throughout my entire career, but even my ugliness was being trumped by other people's greed and ego. It was like a cold glass of water thrown in my face. The cold blast woke me up to the realities of corporate life—every man and woman was out for themselves. Period, end of story. I, myself, had played that role time and time again, but the outright bitchiness of others was creating a thunderstorm of emotions inside me. It had to be squashed. It became apparent from my own self-destruction—drinking, eating, lashing out, and isolating myself from the world—that I couldn't survive the storm that was about to blow through the organization and me. Something had to change.

Less than a month later, it did—our division of the company was going public. The impending company spin-off promised to make most of senior management very wealthy. The mere thought of it turned leaders, mentors, and supporters into greed mongers and egomaniacs. What was once a close-knit, caring organization instantly became a cold, matter-of-fact, cutthroat company. All bets were off and it was every man and woman for themselves.

Donald was right. I was too logical, and that logic was getting the best of me. I wanted no part of the new attitude that the company and its leaders were taking on. After all those years of being a bitch in black suits and high heels, I now wanted to be cooperative and helpful. I wanted to see all of us work together and succeed. I no longer wanted to sabotage others for my own agenda, greed, and ambition.

I was beginning to realize that it was hard to go it alone. I wanted desperately for people to support and follow me because they wanted to, not because they were afraid not to. As a female executive, it was becoming important to me that women work together, not against each other. There were so few executive positions available for women, and the clawing and positioning for them was ruthless. Until women learn how to seek mentors and supporters and form their own "girls' club," the door will be slammed on them and the claws will remain drawn.

I took a hard look at my reflection in the mirror one morning and saw Satan, Ron, and Beth in myself. I didn't like it.

It wasn't their attacks against me; I could handle that. I believed the Biblical Scripture which states, "If God is for me, who could be against me?" And besides, I had little, if any, respect for them. Their attacks rolled right off me. I was seeing myself in them for the first time and it was ugly. I was ashamed of it. Finally I was pursuing an initiative in which I truly believed in and was passionate about. I was going about it truthfully, openly, for the first time in many years. Yet, they never saw that. If they did, they would never admit to it. My mentor and confidant didn't see it, nor would he support me. Instead, he turned his back on me. That thought brought me to tears.

Staring at my reflection, I noticed for the first time the scowl of my mouth, the hardness in my eyes, and the rigidness in my body. It was disturbing. The once foxy, flakey, and far-out girl was unrecognizable. Right then, I wanted to shed the ugliness, curtness, and bitterness that possessed me.

When I returned to Atlanta, I was refreshed and recharged, but this time, my bitch was not reloaded. My desire to fight was drained. My claws were retracted. My tongue was still. My belief in the project and its purpose never wavered, but I no longer wanted to swim with the sharks. I still heard my father's voice telling me to sink or swim. Though I would never sink, I wanted to swim in calmer waters. My soul begged for it. Life wasn't going to make it that easy on me.

A couple of months later, Donald moved on to his next promotion, as did the initiative I had poured my heart and soul into. If I said I wasn't disappointed, I'd be lying. For the first time in my whole life, I felt a small twinge of failure. Then I remembered something I once read: *"When God takes something from your grasp, He's not punishing you, but merely opening your hands to receive something better."* I had finally decided I deserved better.

Worse yet, Donald's new position in Marketing was Ron's old position. Ron's new job was to oversee both the Sales and Consulting organizations. That meant he was now my boss. Each day I waited for the hammer to come down. I knew it was just a matter of time; I just didn't know when. The first pounding came when I was assigned to report to Doug. I was no longer a direct line to senior management. The end was certainly nearing.

Avoiding and ignoring any interaction with Ron, I worked on automating the professional services methodology we used to implement our tools and solutions, and servicing our clients. I couldn't tell you what we accomplished or struggled with during this time. I still felt like a zombie in every aspect of my work and life.

Experts might have diagnosed it as clinical depression, but I considered myself too strong-minded to fall victim to that. For me, it was payback for the tireless years, months, days and hours I gave to the company. I deserved to lie on the couch day after day, fail to respond to calls or emails, relinquish responsibilities to others, and simply check out. *It's the least they could do for the hell they put me through this past year,* I kept telling myself.

My teenage dream of smashing through the glass ceiling was gone. I was losing my desire to fight the politics, agendas, and motives that came with high-powered initiatives of big corporations. I would leave those fights to the Beths, Rons, and Donalds of the world. I longed for so much more.

The remainder of 2007 was a blur. My passions died and the zombie evolved into a robot. I did what I needed to do to get through the day, and no more. For the first time in my entire life, the flame of corporate ambition, success, fame, and all of its toys, burned out. I was exhausted by the storm brewing within me, a struggle between who I was and who I wanted to be. I simply wanted to turn over and go back to sleep until the storm passed.

On November 27, 2007, Doug helped me win that struggle. He gave me my walking papers and my independence. He freed the bitch, the zombie, the *robot*. Walking out the doors that day giggling, I knew that it would take every ounce of determination and potentially every dollar of my life savings, before I would see the walls of another corporation. Corporate didn't bring me to that conclusion. The company didn't even convince me of that. I found that certainty and clarity through the torment and bitch that I put myself and others through. I decided that if I was going to continue to work my ass off like I always had, it was going to be on my terms, in my way.

The moment I walked out the doors of the company, the phones fell silent. I don't know why but I was shocked no one from my so called corporate family reached out to me, including Donald. Surprisingly, Ron emailed me and in his political and cunning way said, "Good luck; sorry it didn't work." I laughed.

That silence taught me an invaluable lesson about business and corporate America. It all boils down to, *'What have you done for me today?'* Nothing else matters. It doesn't matter if you are making them money. It has little significance if you deliver or exceed on projects for the customer or business. Burning the midnight oil and giving up weekends, family vacations, and personal events means little. In fact, it is expected. You have to sacrifice everything and continue to deliver for them or you are at risk. The moment you no longer contribute to the company's success, you are no longer of value.

I don't say this out of bitterness or pain. I loved my corporate life and the teachings, lessons, and best practices it provided me. I owe everything, good and bad, to those twenty-five years. It's just the hard truth that no one waist deep in it wants to see. It's disheartening to me to see our young people forging into the corporate world upon leaving college with the same greedy ambitions, oblivious to what they will have to sacrifice. So many people, me included, work themselves to the bone and give up their personal lives and new adventures — they give up *life* — to chase the corner office. Now, I ask myself, for what?

Though I wasn't aware of it then, that day brought with it the death of my 'bitch' and the beginning of the truly rich life I have now. On that day of independence, the corporate family I had been part of for so long did the best thing any good family member could do; they set me free.

Life's not the breath you take, the breathing in and out
That gets you through the day, ain't what it's all about
Just might miss the point if you don't slow down the pace
Life's not the breaths you take but the moments that take your breath away

George Strait, "Breath You Take"

Chapter 21

THE FACE LIFT

I made my way to the ladies' room on the seventeenth floor of the Georgian Club, paying no mind to the crowd of people leaving the adjoining conference room and heading to the elevator. Suddenly, I got a sixth sense and turned to look at the man waiting for the elevator. An electric shock shot up my spine. The doors opened and he stepped into the elevator. "Wait up!" I yelled, as I ran toward him.

I jumped into the elevator and nearly knocked the poor man down, the man who had handed me my walking papers two years earlier. The man I had walked out on that fateful Monday morning, the day I began to shed the corporate bitch. "Doug!" I squealed with delight.

"Bernadette! What are you doing here?" he asked, shocked to see me.

"I'm a member. And you?" His eyes widened, surprised by my response.

"I sat in on a presentation they were offering," he replied.

The Georgian Club, a private business and social club, held frequent breakfast and lunch presentations and brown bag training sessions. "Oh, that's nice," I said.

The look on his face was priceless. I wished I'd had a camera to snap a picture.

"How are you, and how's everything at the old homestead?" I asked, upbeat. It appeared that nothing had changed since I had been gone. His voice conveyed boredom, something I knew nothing about since the day I ventured out on my own.

"You look great!" he said.

"Thank you," I replied.

I did look great, and I knew it. I had peace in my soul and it showed. I had no anger nor resentment. I had shed the corporate bitch, though like any obsession or addiction, kicking it for good would take time and practice. I knew that.

We talked for a few minutes and I told him to say hello to the old gang. I wished him well, turned, and walked to my car. I was standing tall with my shoulders back and chest out. I knew that the risk I took that day to drive out of that corporate parking lot for the last time and the decision not to look for another high-paying job, with a big office and big title, was considered ludicrous by many of my friends. But for me, it was meant to be. A couple of months later, during a run in the park, I ran into another of my former, corporate peers. Dripping with sweat, I leaned over to rest my hands on my thighs.

"Bernadette?" the familiar voice called out.

Recognizing my former colleague, I said, "Hi Melinda, how are you?"

I had not seen Melinda for three or four years, as she had left the company before me. "I'm great, thanks. How about you?" she asked.

"I feel great, though you wouldn't know that by looking at me now!" I laughed.

"What's new?" she asked.

"How much time do you have?" I joked. It's funny how someone you haven't seen in years will ask that, as if a single sentence or even two can update them on everything that has happened in your life since the last time you saw each other. I told her I had left the company, started my own business, and begun to pursue other opportunities. I was pumped with adrenaline, and Melinda could see it.

"Wow, how exciting!" she said. Then she paused and asked, hesitantly, "You look great, too. Did you have some work done?"

I burst out laughing. "Shedding your bitch makes for one hell of a face lift, doesn't it?" I quipped. "Thanks for noticing!" We both got a big laugh from that.

She brought me up to speed on her life, her latest job, family issues, and how running helps her escape from it all. We hugged each other and promised to stay in touch, even though we both knew we wouldn't. That's okay; I've learned that quality relationships are better than quantity of contacts.

It was motivating and inspiring to hear old friends comment on my emotional face lift. "What happened and what's different?" they would ask. Recently, someone even asked what my, "Aha!" moment was.

"What do you mean?" I asked. I never considered it as an "Aha!" moment. To Rebecca, there must have been.

"Interesting question," I replied. I knew exactly what it was. "It was the heart attack I thought I was having one day, after dealing with fellow bitches at work. I was so disgusted over their behavior, I couldn't take it. Then I realized I was the same way. My blood pressure immediately spiked, my heart raced out of control, my face began to sweat, and my breathing became labored. I thought I was having a heart attack. I decided I wanted nothing to do with creating such strain, negativity, anger, and bitterness. I hated myself and that freaked me out."

"Wow," she replied.

When I left the halls of Corporate America, I became a student again. Not just a student of starting, managing, and growing my own business, but a student of *me*. Each day, I devoted time to focus on learning about who I was, why I was, and who I truly wanted to be. I dug deep into my soul to consider all of the things—good, bad, ugly, hurtful, funny, happy, and special—that I had deposited into my own life and into the lives of others, from the '3-F' sister and insecure romancer, to the competitive athlete and covert operator, to the strategic thinker and the bitch. I looked at it all.

What I learned is that it was the little things in life that brought me the most joy, not the materialistic things I was so obsessed with. It was my moments with family and friends, not my houses, cars, or wardrobes. It was the Christmas Eve midnight mass when I held my youngest brother, Britt, in my arms as he slept. It was the high school recital when I gazed up at my sister Peggy, belting out the songs of *Funny Girl* and felt goose bumps running up and down my arms. The day my little sister, Patricia, got married and the day she asked me to be her first child's godmother. And, of course, the day I stood in the birthing room when that child, Marygrace, was born. The days I sat at my father's bedside, reading passages from our Paris trip journal, while he prepared to die just like he always wanted—at home, surrounded by his wife and children. It was the moment I met my four-legged best friend, Charlie. His sweet face and wet kisses won my heart the instant I saw him.

Looking in the mirror, a few years earlier, I saw the reflection of a woman I no longer recognized and didn't like. That reflection stirred up a great deal of desperation within me, desperation to rediscover the precocious, sassy, and happy girl I had been. I ached for the laughter that came from the gut and the joy from a child's smile. The day I noticed the rainbow following a rain storm or the warm sunshine that filled the clear, blue skies of fall. Although these things had always existed in the world around me, I had never appreciated them.

Those realizations brought me to tears on many occasions, but not as much as one morning when I faced down my fear of receiving and pangs of unworthiness. It was a 'come to Jesus' exchange that changed me forever.

Having spent the last year or so on my personal development journey, I turned my attention to my professional growth. Wanting to up my game and the business I was establishing, I joined a worldwide entrepreneurial private business development club, CEO SPACE. It was a club I was convinced would provide me the education, mentoring, network, and overall challenge that would take my business and me as a leader to the next level. I never expected that it would also propel me emotionally, spiritually, and personally.

My first club 'forum' was in July of 2009. I, along with four hundred other entrepreneurs, prepared for the intense, nine-day curriculum of training, coaching, networking, and prospecting. From seven in the morning until midnight, we were engaging, collaborating, and sharing with each other the skills, talents, and expertise we would need to move our businesses and our lives forward. A core philosophy of the club was to put your agendas aside and give what you could to others. It was as easy as asking someone, "What are you working on, and what do you need next?" Their belief was that in turn, you get what you need.

It might have been their belief, but I didn't trust that it would actually happen. My lifelong experience had been that very few people, if any, truly put aside their agenda and selflessly give to others. Corporate life certainly doesn't train or groom you to give. *I will have to see it to believe it*, I convinced myself.

I, personally, struggled with adopting this whole new philosophy. I came to the forum with specific goals and objectives for my business and I expected to accomplish them. There were people I wanted to meet and things I wanted to learn. In my instilled corporate fashion, I established specific measurements for success to justify the investment. There was a ROI I was determined to make. *What do they mean I have to put my agenda aside?* I thought to myself. *I'll never succeed doing that!*

My competitive streak ran so deeply though me that after five days of giving, I was boiling over with selfishness and greed. For an instant that morning, the old me, the bitchy me, took over. I immediately squashed those thoughts but not before tears were streaming down my face.

The morning of the sixth day, I sat in the forum ballroom wallowing in self-pity. *I have helped so many people*, I thought. *Why wasn't anyone helping me?* I sat there like a boulder, unable to move or be moved.

The Chairman of the organization, Berny Dorhmann, addressed the crowd. He asked the crowded room one simple question that altered my life forever, "Who in the room is stuck in accomplishing the goals you came with?" *Wow*, I thought to myself. *That is a loaded question.* Tears welled up in my eyes.

The old Bernadette, the corporate, masked, and proud Bernadette, would never raise her hand to that question. I would never admit to anyone that I needed something or had failed to achieve my goals. *It certainly would never have happened in front of four hundred people.* But the new Bernadette felt deserving of help and in order to find it, she would have to ask for it.

As quickly as he asked the question, my hand shot up in the air. Berny flagged me and several other brave souls to the front of the room. I took a deep breath, stood, and proudly walked to the front of the room with my head up, shoulders back, and chest out. I stood right next to Berny, unsure of what was coming next.

He turned to the roomful of people and said, "Okay, now it's your turn. These men and women are stuck and need all of your help. I want each of you to ask each of them; what are you working on, and what do you need next. And we don't leave this room until each of them has received what they need."

I stood there shaking and breathing deeply.

Suddenly, the roomful of people jumped out of their seats and ran down the aisle toward me, descending on me with outstretched arms. *Oh my God*, I gasped. As the first person reached me and hugged me close to them, I sank into their arms and balled my eyes out. Miraculously, seconds later the tears were gone. The sunken pit in my stomach was full. Maybe it was one of my 'God's speaking moments,' because suddenly I felt at peace. I felt safe. I shared with them freely what I needed and how they could help. My circle of new friends began handing me business cards and contact sheets with scribbles of people, businesses, and resources specific to my requests.

By the time the roomful of people made their way to me with their selfless compassion and support, the armor of unworthiness and feelings of not deserving, was gone. I freely accepted their help and felt truly deserving of their giving. From that day forward, the philosophy of paying forward, giving, and working cooperatively with others fueled me and everything I did. It especially influenced my relationships, partnerships, and businesses. I was a new woman and leader. It took my breath away.

With five words most people fear, *"You are being let go"*, I let go of the 'bitch'. I rediscovered me and the woman I wanted to be. I thought about the true loves, laughs, adventures, and challenges I had missed out on and grew sad. I realized that the personas and masks I had taken on not only covered up my insecurities, inferiorities, and intimidations, but they had also inhibited my ability to truly love, laugh, and thrill in life's little wonders. Though the initial admission of that cut my heart like a knife, I was exhilarated to have been given a second chance.

Holly had seen it as hysteria when I sat in her living room and laughed with delight that I had just lost my six-figure job and all the perks. A couple of my sisters saw it as denial. Many of my old colleagues thought I was crazy for walking away from everything I had worked so hard for. Finally, I didn't care what other people thought. I was happy, I was free, and I was definitely finding out who I was.

Recently, a marketing agency executive asked me to describe the feeling of 'shedding' I experienced the morning I was let go. Giggling, I said, "It felt like the Wicked Witch of the West in *The Wizard of Oz,* when the bucket of water was thrown in her face. All the ugliness, fear, intimidation, and insecurity melted away, leaving me standing free, open, and real in the sunlight."

I could have said it was like the caterpillar that had shed its cocoon and turned into a beautiful butterfly. Quite honestly, that is way too "fru-fru" for me, too soft and fluffy. It's also too final. It doesn't take into account the process of self-discovery that started that day and continues today. People often ask me, "What's different now?" I simply chuckle and say, "What isn't?!"

I know now that it isn't enough to have great skills and talents; you also have to have the confidence and positive mindset to use them.

I am deserving of what I have if I achieve it through hard work, helping others, and respecting people for what they bring to the table.

I don't know everything and deserve the help and support of other people.

I don't need or want to control everything..... It is what it is. Life's angst, inconveniences and attitude rolling off my back and it is the most exhilarating feeling.

I love to smile and have the people around me smile back. It ignites a flame on my heart.

The last few years have indeed been a second chance for me. A chance to pursue the life I dreamt of as a young girl and to pursue it as the sassy, precocious, confident woman I am.

I'm still driven by big dreams and big goals, but they are based on my passions, my charity, and my ability to influence and impact the world in a positive way. It is no longer based on competitive, greedy, or bitchy motives. What I was, the people I hurt, and the opportunities I missed out on cannot be undone. I have to live with that. I do live with that. Who and what I was all those years gave me a new perspective on who I can be and who I want to be. It was God's plan that I learn them.

Now, I can apologize for my bad behavior and learn from those experiences to inform, inspire, and educate others. I can bathe in honey, not the vinegar I had poured onto every situation in my life.

People may look at my life and believe that being a bitch worked for me and they wouldn't be wrong. I was successful. But it came with an emotional, spiritual, and physical price, one that had me gasping for air more than once. It left me curled up on the ground in the park that day with the realization of the cruelty and hurt I had inflicted on so many people. I added hatred and pain to the world where there is already too much ugliness. That was not the real me and this world deserves to know the real me! I deserve to be the real me!

When I went to Las Vegas to promote this book, I brought a large poster board image of the book cover. I set it up in the hallway of my hotel to draw people into my room to hear my marketing presentation. One day, I overheard young girls laughing outside my room.

"Hey girls, can I help you?" I asked.

Two of the teenagers from the entrepreneurship program I was participating in walked in hesitantly, giggling.

"What's up?" I asked.

"We like your poster," one of them said. "I like being a bitch."

"You do?" I asked, incredulous.

"Sure, it helps me get what I want," she explained.

Wow, I thought. *That is what the world is teaching our young girls and boys.* Turn on any television show and you'll see that being a bitch is considered acceptable, intriguing, and cool.

My motherly instincts called out for me to lecture them on the consequences of being a bitch. Instead, I asked, "Girls, do you think that if there was something you really wanted, and you negotiated fairly and with respect, you could still get what you want?" They looked lost.

"Does that make sense?" I asked.

"Yes!" one girl replied.

"But it's fun," the other, younger, girl said. I resisted the urge to take them by the shoulders and shake them.

"Girls, take it from a former bitch," I said. They laughed. "The only reason a guy or girl acts like a bitch and treats people like dirt, is because they lack the confidence to use their skills or talent to get what they want by being themselves." The girls began to squirm. *I hit a nerve*, I thought.

"Girls, bitches are covering up insecurity. They doubt themselves in some way so they disguise it by being rude, curt, and obnoxious," I continued. They both shrugged and quietly walked out of the room. I listened for their giggles but heard complete silence.

I was no different from those two girls. Years earlier, I consciously and purposely took on the persona of a bitch because I thought that it would get me what I wanted. I abandoned my confidence in my skills and talents and decided that being a bitch was the way to be successful. Anyone who met me would never have come to that conclusion. They only saw a strong, confident, and influential woman. Adopting my parent's philosophy, what they didn't know didn't hurt them.

Since my day of independence in 2007, I've spent a great deal of time analyzing why, when, who, and what caused me to believe those things to the point of changing who I was. I can take myself back to those feelings of being 'different', not fitting in with my own family, and feeling like an outsider of any group I wanted to be a part of. I can recall the intimidation I felt from my father's high expectations, and the uncertainty that I deserved what I earned. Sometimes, it feels like it was yesterday. Other times it feels like an out-of-body experience. I still work on myself to accept that I deserve and am worthy of great things in life.

I relive those feelings and emotions so I truly understand and take accountability for the reason I was such a bitch: *I allowed myself to become one!!!!*

No one ever told me I wasn't good enough or that I didn't fit in. No one ever told me I couldn't accomplish whatever I wanted. No one ever told me I was not worthy of their love or anyone else's love. I told myself these things. I did not believe in me.

The best part of coming to terms with my past is that it has taken years off my body, my mind, and my face. Shedding my corporate bitch gave me a mental and emotional face lift.

"If your actions inspire others to dream more, learn more, do more and become more, you are a leader."

—John Quincy Adams

Chapter 22

TODAY'S REFLECTION IN THE MIRROR SHIFTING FROM BITCH TO RICH!

It's been three years since my Independence Day and I am happier than ever. I took all the strengths, skills, and talents that made me successful as an intrapreneur and jumped off the cliff into entrepreneurship. With my years of retail, business, and management experience—and deep pockets (thanks to my corporate career savings)—I started a business management and consulting firm to help small business owners become more productive and efficient.

A born risk taker, I started my business in 2008, despite the recession, fear, and closed wallets. I am often asked what possessed me to start my own business in the worst economic times that we have ever seen. Once I control my giggles, I reply, "Because I could." I wasn't forced to go out on my own, as the job market had not yet collapsed. I just never considered looking for a job, or what is better known as 'just over broke'. Even though my corporate life ended in such an ugly way, my years in the trenches armed me with great skills and talents, which I continue to rely on today.

In 2010, I started a second business, where I use my own 'bitch' lessons to educate, inform, and motivate other women and men to shed their negative attitudes, mindsets, and belief systems and learn to live their richest lives. I thought, *Who better than a reformed bitch to train, educate, and motivate corporate executives and teams on how to handle difficult conversations in the workplace? Who better to teach them how to negotiate, collaborate, and engage with one another and to use their skills and talents in pursuit of their goals? Who better to encourage them to ultimately believe in themselves against all odds?*

Starting my own businesses is the most challenging, empowering, and risky thing I've ever done. I'm now fully responsible for putting food on my table, keeping a roof over my head and clothes on my back. When asked by many laid off and employed corporate employees if I would choose to start my own business if I were fired again today, I say, "Absolutely!" As scary as it can be, the fact that you control what you do, with whom you do it, and how, why, and when you do it, is exciting. Is it a risk? Absolutely, but what fun would life be without risk?

Managing my own business has also changed my perspective on what it takes to run a corporation. It's hard! There are many days I sit in my home office looking over my pages of to-do's and wish I could click my heels together a few times and have people, resources, and money show up. Instead, I use all of the skills and talents I learned from my corporate days— negotiating, organization, planning, and partnering—to minimize the effort.

Gone with my days of corporate life were the competitive culture I thrived on, the cowboy approach to delivering projects, and the uptight, strict, and politically correct way I worked with employees, partners, vendors, and customers. In my own businesses, I am very transparent about how we do business, who we do business with, and at what cost. I focus on creating partnerships and alliances with people who provide skills I lack. I surround myself with employees, partners, coaches, and advisors who are smarter than I am. I also leverage what I learned from those years:

- *Delivering top quality service and great value to my customers*
- *Working myself to the bone to meet deadlines and budgets*
- *Under-estimating and over-delivering*
- *Forming alliances and partnerships that fill gaps and extend capabilities and offerings*
- *Dressing to impress (just not in manly, starched shirts and dark suits)*

From the first day of owning my own business, I was determined to never put on a dark suit or dress again. More specifically, I wanted to shed more than my bitch; I wanted to purge my wardrobe of anything black and structured, replacing it with color and fluidity.

In October 2009, during my second forum with CEO SPACE, I met image therapist Liana Chaouli, whose work teaches clients how to make their fashion sense congruent with what is in their soul. She is a CEO SPACE instructor and coach and spent a great deal of time with forum members helping them to express their voice through their wardrobe. She was the exact person I needed to help me with my transformation. One evening, when the last class broke up, I ran to the dining room to grab an empty seat at her table. Fortunately, she was already seated when I nabbed a chair.

Desperate for one-on-one time with her, I immediately asked her how she could help me shed my standard, conservative, black corporate look. She smiled and laughed, and asked me some questions that made me instantly uncomfortable: "*What size family do you have? Where are you in the lineup of kids? What is your relationship like with your father? Are you in a relationship?*" I was caught off guard but answered the questions as seriously as she asked them. Finally, she asked, "When was the last time you were in a relationship?"

When I answered, she paused and asked, "Why? Are you gay?"

"No," I replied, wondering where she was going with all this. I began to get emotional and uncomfortable with what was about to happen.

The table began to fill up with other members wanting her assistance. Leaning in toward me from across the table, she stated, matter-of-factly, "Bernadette, you have one of the strongest personalities I have ever met. It makes sense that you are your father's seventh son. When you walk into a room, everyone knows you are here. It wouldn't surprise me that you scare the hell out of men and women."

In front of the entire table, tears poured down my face, again. *I have never cried as much as I did these past few years*, I thought to myself. She asked why I was getting so emotional. Fighting back the tears, I said, "I am so tired of people saying I intimidate them, or scare them. I want to be soft, feminine, loved." I am not sure who sat next to me, but they wrapped their arm around my shoulder. I went on to tell her about this very book about shedding the bitch I had been. I told her it was the exact reason I wanted to speak to her: to learn how to introduce color into my life and attract, rather than repel, people.

"I understand, but you aren't ready," she said. "Continue writing, continue discovering who you are, and then you will be open to new things. Right now, I can attempt to put you in soft colors and fabrics, but you will make excuses for why they don't work. Trust me. Continue digging and writing, then let's meet in December, and we will see where you are," she said.

I was devastated. Not because the conversation played out at a table full of strangers. It wasn't because she was telling me that I was not ready. It was because she was right. I was still holding back on revealing the true me. I was still scared and distrusting of what other people thought of me. *For years I was so nasty to people. Can that really go away overnight?* I wondered.

It felt safer to be clothed in what comforted me, what protected me, what was familiar to me. Here, all this time, I was running away from my old life, but I still had so far to go. When I returned home, I spent more time with people asking them for their help in my self-excavation. I asked them for their perceptions, advice, and impressions. I listened, asked questions, and evaluated how to use the knowledge for growth.

In December, when I returned to the forum and to Liana's table, we talked for an hour about the transformation that had been taking place. We scheduled time in her forum showroom. By the time we were done, I walked out with beautiful purple, teal, and green, flowy dresses, shoes, and dangling jewelry. When I wore them, I owned them and the woman I had become. The reaction from my forum friends was priceless. The smiles on their faces confirmed for me that I was on the right path to finding my '3-F' girl again.

I hadn't just shed the bitch; I had shed the black dresses and pant suits, too. For good!

Throughout my transformation, I would have had a lot of sleepless nights, were it not for my faith in God, prayer, belief in myself, and a strong support system. Each morning, before jumping out of bed to take on the day, I stop, pull Charlie to me, close my eyes, and spend time thanking God for all my blessings, and asking Him for guidance, protection, and love. My favorite prayers are those my parents loved—the Our Father and Hail Mary, and mine, the Prayer of Jabez.

I have observed and learned these past few years that the happiest, most successful people are those who have an unshakable faith in God. As I pursued training and self-development courses, I noticed that the people I met, young and old, well-known and unknown, attributed their success to faith and prayer. Never one to wear my faith on my sleeve, I turned away from them, uncomfortable at first. But after awhile, it was hard to ignore and deny the role faith and God has played in my life. It's what gives me the confidence that I'll have a rich, prosperous, and successful life no matter the challenges and adversities I may face along the way.

When someone asks how I was able to walk away from the security of my job without ever turning back, I simply say, "Faith!"

As I continued to evolve and grow, my real friends revealed themselves and my not-so-true friends fell by the wayside. I let go of unhealthy friends who didn't believe in me or support my dreams. I no longer wanted anyone or anything in my life that was angry, mean, negative, unsupportive, or bitchy. I only wanted people in my life who were loyal, honest, and willing to confront me and call me out in a positive way.

My circle of friends became very small and at times, completely empty. There were many nights I spent alone at home, with just Charlie to keep me company. Still, I've never been calmer, happier, or more at peace.

As I began to let my walls down, I began to flirt again and became more open to advances from potential suitors. Over time, new friends appeared, friends who would be my cheerleaders, coaches, and challengers. They motivate me and give themselves unselfishly so that I might find success in this new chapter in my life.

My family continues to shower me with their love, support, and encouragement, as they always have. When any one of us faces hardships, we are all there for each other. As I type these words, my mother rests in a hospital, her children surrounding her. Because I am still the only one away from home, they comfort me regularly with phone calls, emails, and Facebook postings. Somehow, when I need them, the phone rings and my mother or one of my siblings announces, "We're coming down for a visit!" Each time it happens, I think, *They must have had their own "God's speaking" moment. He told them I need them.*

Today, I measure success not by bank accounts, fancy cars, and beautiful houses, but by the happiness I'm able to experience and share with others. I work tirelessly on my business, and though it can be a roller coaster at times, it is always exciting. I'm thrilled when people who meet me say they could never see me as a bitch. It always makes me giggle, because when I look in the mirror, I can't see it, either.

I love the bold and audacious woman I am. I feel like my ten year-old self again, only more mature and refined. My spirit, mind, body, and heart are pure and I feel elated and free. My new mantra, "It is what it is," stops me in my tracks when dealing with life's inconveniences. I have learned to smell the roses while handling the thorns with calm and confidence.

I'm still single, never married, though now I am open to risking my heart. I know that feeling something, even hurt, is better than feeling nothing at all. My family of siblings, in-laws, nieces, and nephews remain my greatest source of strength and pride. My small circle of true and loyal friends and colleagues empower me. Although I do have hereditary high blood pressure, I am physically fit, healthy, and active, and accept and love my body the same way I love my heart. My four-legged best friend, Charlie, helps keep me young. He brought out the child in me and reminded me what giddy, unconditional love feels like. Now, I welcome it in all areas of my life.

I've spent a lot of time not only reflecting on those bitchy days, but acknowledging my role in the way they played out. It was painful, even gut-wrenching at times, to take a hard look in the mirror and be completely honest with myself. I avoided it for more than twenty-five years. Yet, within days of being fired from my corporate job, I went to work, staring intently at my own reflection. Ready, willing and armed with boxes of tissues, I sat down night after night, with a fresh journal and a new black pen, delving into my soul, searching for answers to the following questions:

- *What specific things, emotions, or situations created my bitch?*
- *Would I have been just as, or even more, successful not being a bitch?*
- *Did I lose my career-long mentor because of my bitch?*
- *Did I lose my job because of corporate changes or because of my bitch?*
- *Could I have broken that glass ceiling had I never become a bitch?*

What role did my attitude have on my love life and my friendships?

Many of the answers stung, and several shocked me. But when I faced them, the sting subsided and a stronger woman emerged from the pain.

My 'bitch' was created, in part, by the influences around me, but mostly by the insecurities, inferiorities, and inadequacies I allowed to seep into my soul as a young girl. Childish jabs and teasing and unwanted advances took hold of my mind and soul and didn't let go for a long time. Though others thought they were small and trivial at the time, for me, they were life-changing. I became a bitch through my own choosing. I allowed childhood taunts and misconceptions to take root in my psyche and abuse me emotionally. It was a terrible way to live, and I wouldn't wish it on anyone.

I'd be lying if I denied my responsibility for losing my mentor and coach. Did his greed and ego contribute to it? Maybe, but I have learned that if I want something to change, I have to change. I didn't understand that then. As a bitch, I believed that everyone else needed to adapt to me. I wasn't about to change for anyone, including Donald. Had I changed, would I have lost our partnership? Probably not.

Did I lose my job for being a bitch? I would have to say, "Absolutely." I won't even blame Ron or organizational changes, as easy as it is to do. He knows his part in it, just as he knew why he didn't want me playing in his sand box. I did not fit their mold. Bitches don't fit many company molds, no matter how skilled and talented they are. Underneath the mask, they lack the confidence, mindset, and belief in themselves to leverage those skills and talents.

Today, large and small businesses engage me to help them find a solution to breaking the glass ceiling for the women in their organization. On one particular call, a man who headed up a large medical practice explained to me how the two women on his Board of Directors, both eligible to replace the CEO, were going to be overlooked, because, he stated, "They're bitches." The women were qualified and deserving of the position, but no one would vote them in because of their attitudes. I knew exactly what he was dealing with.

He asked me for some solutions on how to handle it. I explained to him that unfortunately, it was a common situation in many companies. There isn't an evening out at corporate or entrepreneurial events where I don't hear women complaining about each other, the glass ceiling, the boys' club, and the politics that are preventing them from breaking through. The men I meet complain about how they continue to try to promote and advocate for women, but they make it hard to do so. Women aren't facing the reality of their actions, and men are not willing to confront them.

We discussed various options, including 360 degree assessments, company-wide workshops and presentations, or tough love straight talk. I explained how I love being in the position to admit to my own bitch so I can help other women shed their own. He gasped and admitted, "I'd prefer to just ignore it."

So do most people in Corporate America. Unfortunately, women don't realize it. Men avoid both the issue and the women, companies ignore training or mentoring women, and women don't attempt to help each other—the one thing they can do. Women complain that men have their boys' club, yet few women attempt to form their own girls' club. When they do, women bring their competitiveness, emotions, and drama with them. Men can compete, negotiate, fight with one another, and then turn around and share a beer. Women have not learned to do the same. I know. I was that woman.

I worked hard to show up the other women around me. I fought to win the promotions and new projects over them. I wanted to be the best-dressed, most decorated, and most involved woman. I wanted to be the first woman to successfully break the glass ceiling. It pained me when I admitted to myself that it wasn't going to happen as long as I did not cooperate, collaborate, engage, support, mentor, and lead other women and men into those same positions.

Here are some of the biggest lessons I learned from being the bitch I was and the rich woman I am now:

- *Women owe it to themselves to NOT be like men, but to learn from them!*

- *Form alliances, mastermind groups, and girls' clubs to engage, collaborate, mentor, and support each other.*

- *Encourage and promote other women, openly and graciously, without any ulterior motive or agenda.*

- *Learn to not wear your emotions on your sleeve. If you have to, learn to manage them with a thick skin, rather than create drama.*

- *Use the natural talents and skills that make women unique and special— nurturing, caring, intuitive, and dedicated.*

- *Say 'no' and set boundaries as to what you are willing to do to get ahead. Use your confidence to stand up for yourself and not be taken advantage of.*

The bottom line is that women will continue to be overlooked until companies, male leaders, and women themselves decide to do something about it. Women need to stop complaining about what isn't happening. They need to be the ones to change and make things happen. They can't accept the norm. They need to take risks, trust in themselves, and leverage their confidence along with their skills and talents to pursue the dreams and goals they have.

Women don't need to 'man up,' be part of the boys' club, or bitch their way to the top. Women just need to be strong, confident, assertive, dedicated, risk-taking, and dignified. Period.

Male business leaders and companies have a role to play, as well. They need to support, mentor, and coach women (and men) to leverage their talents, skills, and confident mindsets. Where women lack confidence, leaders and companies need to motivate and support them. They need to confront their people, guide them, and lead them. Women are begging for engagement, involvement, and collaboration. They want to be real but often are not—because corporate America forces them to be something else. No one wins by avoiding, ignoring, or overlooking bitchy women.

I am often asked what I would do differently if I were to live my corporate life over again. Here is my short list. I would:

- *Show up each and every day as me, Bernadette. No one else.*

- *Seek out male and female coaches and mentors who I respected and admired for their own leadership styles.*

- *Be a lifelong student, both professionally and personally. If I lacked the skills and talents I would seek them out. If I had insecurities, intimidations, or doubts of any kind, I would seek support, experience, and challenges to overcome them.*

- *Remember that angst, attitude, and bitchiness are merely cover-ups of something else that is lacking. I would do the internal work, even if it was painful, to find out what was lacking and fix it.*

- *Never compromise on who I am and what I believe in, no matter what!*

That is what I would do differently. But because life is meant to be lived forward, I can only hold fast and learn to embrace the lessons I've learned and the wisdom important people have given me throughout my life. It is my pleasure and privilege to share some of these insights with you in hopes that I can help you shed your own bitch, whatever it might be, so you, too, can realize the true riches of life:

- *You can sink or swim!*
  - ♦ *Always choose to swim, regardless of the tide or the conditions of the water. You can always wear a safety vest!*

- *Laugh at yourself!*
  - ♦ *Just as my father chanted, "Oh, wa, ta na, si am!" Learn to not take things so personally or intensely. Allow mistakes, mishaps, and embarrassments roll off your back.*
  - ♦ *If you can't laugh at yourself, you miss out on appreciating who you really are.*

- *There is a right time and place for everything.*
  - ♦ *Don't get pissed or hurt if you are overlooked; just know that it wasn't your time.*
  - ♦ *Have faith in who you are and what you are capable of and it will happen, when it is supposed to happen.*

- *Don't go it alone.*
  - ♦ *Create a support system of family, true friends, and mentors that want only the best for you!*
  - ♦ *Form girl clubs and masterminds with other women that can provide insight into business, office politics, your goals, leadership and more importantly support and motivation.*

- *Fire anyone who is bad for business or for you.*
  - ♦ *Let go of anyone in your life who doesn't support, inspire, and motivate you toward your dreams. Anyone!*
  - ♦ *Don't allow toxic individuals to bring you down with them. You deserve better!*

- *Keep in mind - The grass isn't greener on the other side.*
  - ♦ *Consider Oprah…regardless of the billions she has, she openly admits to the struggles that she has had in her life.*

- ♦ *Compromising who YOU are in order to be Oprah (or anyone else), and to possess materialistic things; money, cars, the big corner office, does NOT guarantee success. YOU guarantee success!*

- *If you work hard you **do** DESERVE to earn whatever you want!*

- *It is what it IS!!!!*

  - ♦ *Let go of controlling your life. It is far more exciting not knowing what tomorrow will bring!*

  - ♦ *Let the small inconveniences of life roll off of your back. The angst they create only stresses you, they don't enhance you. Let them go.*

- *Don't settle for easy! Strive for challenge, risk, and growth.*

- *Take risks, be innovative and creative, and don't let your situation hold you back from stepping out on the edge!*

- *Believe in yourself. God does!*

- *Bottom line - who cares what other people think of you?*

  - ♦ *You have to be happy with you! Don't do anything that compromises who you are. You will be shortchanging yourself.*

  - ♦ *You being YOU is the ULTIMATE SUCCESS.*

  - ♦ *You are who YOU are meant to be!*

Even after all of my internal work, I cannot guarantee that life won't stir up negative thoughts, major angst, attitude, or a bitch in me. I can't even guarantee that I will never depend on Corporate America again. I can say confidently and certainly, that if I am confronted with any of those things again, the woman who will tackle them is a much stronger, bolder, and more audacious woman than I used to be. I will continue to make mistakes and come up short on occasion, but shedding my bitch was the richest thing I could ever do for myself, my family, friends, employees, and customers.

Thank you to all of the people in my life who believed in me, who loved me, and who fought with me. I can now move on to the next chapters of my life. I hope you come along.

THE CORPORATE BITCH TEST

Are you a CORPORATE bitch—hurting both yourself and your career? Do you know?

Take 'The Bitch Test' to find out then commit to SHIFTING from bitch to rich!

Don't be afraid or avoid the result. Remember, knowing yourself clearly will allow you to be who you want to be!

NOTE: once you have completed this self-assessment, you could ask those employees, peers and managers you trust and respect to give you upfront and honest feedback as well. You don't want to find out after you failed to reach your goals.

THE CORPORATE BITCH TEST

Respond YES or NO to each of the following statements. If you answer 'Yes' to one or several of the following statements, you may possess a negative attitude or bitch that is holding you back and keeping you from the riches of life you deserve.

- *Make note of the date you take the assessment*
- *Make note of your responses*
- *Commit to change any Yes responses to No over time.*
- *Come back to the test several months down the road, and reassess.*
- *Focusing on your bitches will help you shed it to obtain riches.*

Outwardly: **YES or NO**

I intimidate or dominate employees, peers and managers   _____

I man-up or act as a bitch in order to compete   _____

I find myself standing alone or avoided at social events   _____

I position myself as if I am better or superior to others   _____

I eat, drink, smoke or have other compulsions   _____

Inwardly:

I am not always convinced I have what it takes   _____

I feel insecure standing up and asking people for things   _____

I don't feel worthy to obtain what I want   _____

I feel angry, uptight, and tense more often than happy   _____

I have a hard time thinking positively about myself   _____

Define your SHIFT PLAN:

Identify your Top 3—YES responses that you want
to shift from bitch to rich in the next 90 days?

_____

_____

_____

List activities you will focus on to achieve your
SHIFT for each of the above—

_____

_____

_____

What RICHES (reward) will you give yourself for achieving your SHIFT?

_____

_____

POST RICHES:

What commitment will you make to create your new YOU now that you
have achieved your SHIFT?

_____

_____

Should you have any questions during your assessment and shift,
visit www.sheddingthecorporatebitch.com
and leave a comment or question or contact us!

MY RICH LIFE IN PICTURES

My Beautiful Parents

The Boas Kids

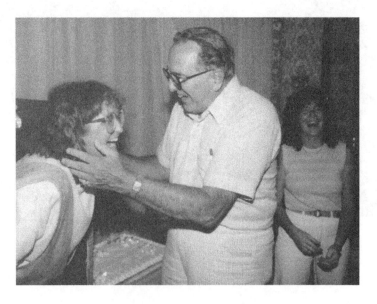

Surprising Dad, a Rarity!

My Hero and My Rock

The Boas Chicks

The Boas Guys

My Confidante, Peggy

My Precious Sister—Patricia

My Heart - Marygrace

My Best Friend—Charlie

ACKNOWLEDGEMENTS

Prayer has always played a significant part in my life. I pray not only to request help, guidance or for forgiveness, but also to say, 'thank you' for the unbelievable blessings I have been given throughout my life—no matter how crazy my life has sometimes been.

One of those blessings has been my family, and I have to thank all of them; my mother, father, and each of my brothers and sisters—Chris, Mark, Mary, Peggy, Theresa, Anne Marie, Matthew, Michael, Jimmy, Patricia and Britt.

I have always been in awe of my mother and father, not because of their fifty-plus year marriage or endless love for one another (though I admire that), but because of the undeniable, unquestionable love and support that they shower on me and every one of my siblings. It is because of all of their support that I have been able to experience the adventures, opportunities, challenges, successes, and failures that I have. No matter what, they are there for me, and that alone gives me the strength and courage to tackle life. I find it hard to describe my exact feelings, as tears are already flowing just thinking about it.

Though my father died in 2005 he is still very much alive in my heart.

We 'Boas kids' don't often call out or favor one person over all the others, but I absolutely have to. I owe my sister, Peggy, for her endless support and tireless contribution to this book, to my business, and to my life. Words cannot adequately express how much I appreciate everything she has done for me.

My circle of friends has changed and gone through its own transformation since I started this project. My dear friend Michelle Fishman has been there for me through it all—thick and thin, tears and laughter. Even though we are physically hundreds of miles away from each other, our twenty-plus year friendship continues to grow, both spiritually and emotionally. I love ya, girl!

I can't go without thanking one of my newest friends, coach and confidante Kay Zurn, who, in the nine short months since we met, has encouraged, challenged, and believed in me, every step of the way.

The story and message within this book would not have been discovered had it not been for the gracious ear of Cassie Parks. Her sincerity allowed me to share my fears and emotions that released the bitch within me.

To Patrick Smyth of TeraGanix, Inc. who shares my passion and vision, and has provided guidance to me throughout the development and growth of both the book and my business.

Nichole Bazemore, my editor, worked tirelessly to ensure my voice and soul shined brightly. When I didn't want to dig any deeper, she pushed and supported me. I thank her for making the very challenging task of writing fulfilling and freeing.

A special thanks to Joyce Curtis, my personal coach, mentor, and friend. Even though our weekly calls would often find me with missed deadlines, unaccomplished goals, or a need for tough love, her gentle manner and inquisitive nature always fueled my spirit. No matter my mood or state of mind, I knew when I hung up the phone I would be focused, energized, and refueled with confidence and determination. She has been a true confidante.

I have always had the great fortune throughout my life to be surrounded by people who believed in me, no matter what. To each and every one of you, thank you! I have always known you can't go through life alone, and though my world may have felt large and engulfing at times, your outstretched hands and hearts always pulled me in close to you.

Thank you!

ABOUT THE AUTHOR

Bernadette Boas is a 'ball of fire' that inspires, motivates and equips individuals and professionals with the mindset, skills, and talents they need to obtain success and prosperity in life.

Leveraging her twenty five years in Corporate America in various consulting, management and leadership roles, Bernadette is a celebrated motivational speaker, shifter and educator, dedicated and determined to change the way leaders are created, and how women and men become movers and shakers toward their life's goals. Bernadette's story, both personal and professional, is humorous and inspirational while providing great insights and lessons to individuals, associations, and corporations.

Bernadette is the founder and CEO of two aspiring Atlanta, Georgia based companies, The Boas Group, a business management consulting practice, and Ball of Fire, Inc., a media, communications and publishing firm,and home of megabrands, Shedding the Bitch™, Creating the Rich......™ and Business Rich Accelerator™, all focused on the health, wealth, and prosperity of individuals and organizations.

Shedding the Corporate Bitch is one in a series of books, training products, events and media in Ball of Fire, Inc.'s, Shedding the Bitch™ brand line that champions individuals to shift all of their life challenges, issues, attitudes and negative mindsets from Bitch to Rich.

To learn more about Shedding the Bitch™ events, training products, and services, as well to obtain additional tools, tips and advice, visit our website at www.sheddingthebitch.com or contact us at:

Ball of Fire, Inc.
Atlanta, Georgia 30318
Email: **BernadetteBoas@BallofFireInc.com**

Join the Shedding the Bitch™ Movement!
By signing up for our monthly RICH Tips!
www.sheddingthebitch.com

and receive our E Book –
Ditch the Bitch or Kill Her With Kindness!
FREE

BUY A SHARE OF THE FUTURE IN YOUR COMMUNITY

These certificates make great holiday, graduation and birthday gifts that can be personalized with the recipient's name. The cost of one S.H.A.R.E. or one square foot is $54.17. The personalized certificate is suitable for framing and will state the number of shares purchased and the amount of each share, as well as the recipient's name. The home that you participate in "building" will last for many years and will continue to grow in value.

Here is a sample SHARE certificate:

HABITAT FOR HUMANITY

THIS CERTIFIES THAT
YOUR NAME HERE
HAS INVESTED IN A HOME FOR A DESERVING FAMILY

1985-2010
TWENTY-FIVE YEARS OF BUILDING FUTURES
IN OUR COMMUNITY ONE HOME AT A TIME

1200 SQUARE FOOT HOUSE @ $65,000 = $54.17 PER SQUARE FOOT
This certificate represents a tax deductible donation. It has no cash value.

YES, I WOULD LIKE TO HELP!

I support the work that Habitat for Humanity does and I want to be part of the excitement! As a donor, I will receive periodic updates on your construction activities but, more importantly, I know my gift will help a family in our community realize the dream of homeownership. **I would like to SHARE in your efforts against substandard housing in my community!** *(Please print below)*

PLEASE SEND ME _____ SHARES at $54.17 EACH = $ $_____

In Honor Of: _____

Occasion: (Circle One) HOLIDAY BIRTHDAY ANNIVERSARY

        OTHER: _____

Address of Recipient: _____

Gift From: _____ *Donor Address:* _____

Donor Email: _____

I AM ENCLOSING A CHECK FOR $ $_____ PAYABLE TO HABITAT FOR HUMANITY OR PLEASE CHARGE MY VISA OR MASTERCARD *(CIRCLE ONE)*

Card Number _____ Expiration Date: _____

Name as it appears on Credit Card _____ Charge Amount $ _____

Signature _____

Billing Address _____

Telephone # Day _____ Eve _____

PLEASE NOTE: Your contribution is tax-deductible to the fullest extent allowed by law.
Habitat for Humanity • P.O. Box 1443 • Newport News, VA 23601 • 757-596-5553
www.HelpHabitatforHumanity.org

www.ingramcontent.com/pod-product-compliance
Lightning Source LLC
Jackson TN
JSHW020017141224
75386JS00025B/570